The White Magic Book

"But, could I buy in this city a book of magic, that were my purchase."
—George Meredith

The White Magic Book

```
+ELOHIM+ELOHI+
 4  14  15   1
 9   7   6  12
 5  11  10   8
16   2   3  13
+ROGYEL+IOSEPHIEL+
```
(ADONAI / ZEBAOTH on sides)

TABLET OF JUPITER

Mrs. John Le Breton
Introduction by Monte Farber

Red Wheel
Boston, MA / York Beach, ME

First published in 2001 by
Red Wheel/Weiser, LLC
P. O. Box 612
York Beach, ME 03910-0612
www.redwheelweiser.com

Introduction copyright © 2001 Monte Farber
All rights reserved. No part of this publication may be reproduced or transmitted
in any form or by any means, electronic or mechanical, including photocopying,
recording, or by any information storage and retrieval system, without permission
in writing from Red Wheel/Weiser, LLC. Reviewers may quote brief passages.

Library of Congress Cataloging-in-Publication Data

Le Breton, John, Mrs.
 The white magic book/Mrs. John Le Breton; Monte Farber, introduction.
   p. cm.
 Originally published: London: C.A. Pearson, 1919. With new introd.
 ISBN 1-59003-004-4 (alk. paper)
   1. Fortune-telling by books. I. Title.

BF1891.B66 L43 2001
133.3--dc21   2001019972

Typeset in Adobe Caslon

Printed in the United States of America

EB

08 07 06 05 04 03 02 01
8 7 6 5 4 3 2 1

The paper used in this publication meets the minimum requirements of the
American National Standard for Information Sciences-Permanence of Paper for
Printed Library Materials Z39.48-1992 (R1997).

Contents

Introduction by Monte Farber...vii

Preface by Mrs. John Le Breton..xix

Introduction by Mrs. John Le Breton...............................xxxiii

Table of Signs and How to Use It.......................................xxxv

Questions...xxxix

Signs Corresponding to the Answers
on Each Page...xliii

Answers..5

Introduction to the 2001 Edition

by Monte Farber

When I was asked to write the introduction to the amazing book you are now holding in your hands, I realized that this was no straightforward proposition. I had a puzzle to solve. I love puzzles. Not jigsaw puzzles, but the kind that make your brain build new neural patterns as you expand your mind to solve them. I love such "games," though I rarely refer to them that way because I respect their power too much. In fact, I invent them. So I am delighted to share with you my discovery of this puzzle, *The White Magic Book*.

This is not merely a book that offers advice about how to make your life one of quality and meaning. (I'm glad to say there are a lot of those.) *The White Magic Book* is just what the title says it is. It is a book of White Magic. So right away there is something quite out of the ordinary that needs to be explained. What is White Magic? And what is a book of White Magic?

White Magic is striving to live in harmony with the scientific principles that create, sustain, and transform our universe without inflicting our desires on anyone who does not want to be a party to them. For example, a practitioner of White Magic might do a prosperity ritual on the New Moon because that time is accepted by farmers to be advantageous for planting seeds, both figuratively and literally. Another example of modern White Magic would be the use of healing

The White Magic Book

touch and visualizations in the healing process using the still mysterious mind/body connection. Practitioners of White Magic are interested in helping and healing both themselves and others. A person can spend a lifetime learning the details of the practice of White Magic. But you really only need pick up a book like this and follow its simple instructions to begin practicing White Magic in your life.

Conversely, Black Magic is the practice of working one's will on the world, but especially on other people, to an end that is not only purely personal, but usually frighteningly and stupidly selfish. All such actions have consequences that ultimately undo any advantages created by their practice and leave the practitioner of Black Magic at least two steps behind where he or she started. Simply put, you can't try to force acorns to grow on apple trees or force someone to "prove" their love for you by filling your every need.

Becoming adept at White Magic involves learning and understanding the underlying principles of our universe. It also involves creating a daily practice that uses those principles in a sort of active meditation. What do I mean by an active meditation? One that allows and encourages the practitioner to actually tap into and make use of his or her powers, both physical and metaphysical (beyond the physical). As long as this power is used for the good of all to the best of one's ability, the manifestations of events, objects, and states of mind will produce harmony and benefit. It's crucial for the White Magic practitioner to be constantly reminded and mindful that the power that is being worked with is not his or her personal property. To that end, this daily practice and reminder must be embodied in a method that is effective, instructive, and enjoyable enough so that the person doing it will use it

The White Magic Book

consistently and enthusiastically. *The White Magic Book*, originally published (as near as we can tell) in 1919, is such an embodiment. To use it on a regular basis, as I'm sure you'll discover, is to be amazed at how well it works and to have fun figuring out its messages to you.

Solving the Puzzle of the White Magic Book

The puzzle isn't solved just because we know what White Magic is and that White Magic is what this book is about. Why has the mysterious Mrs. John Le Breton, whose identity is forever lost to us due to the chauvinistic way women were hidden behind their husbands' names (a practice still in use, I might add), made such curious choices with the design of this book?

Why is This the Tablet of Jupiter?

Why did she choose to use only the seven planets of the astrology of the Middle Ages, i.e., the Sun, the Moon, Mercury, Venus, Mars, Jupiter, and Saturn?

Why does she only use nine of the twelve signs of the astrological zodiac?

Most baffling of all, why does she start the Arabic numbered pages of her book, the ones containing the actual answers to our questions, with the number 5 and not the number 1?

As someone who has studied metaphysics for more than three decades, I believe I know the answers to almost all of these questions. The answers to most of them lie hidden in plain sight. They're on the title page at the front of the book, within what Mrs. Le Breton calls "The Tablet of Jupiter." In astrology, Jupiter symbolizes wisdom, expansion, good fortune.

The White Magic Book

With Jupiter we can think globally, look at the "big picture," and puzzle out answers to the big questions about the meaning and purpose of our lives. Printed in the border of the Tablet are English translations of the Hebrew names of their masculine concept of a Supreme Being and what I believe are Mrs. Breton's names for His Angelic messengers. The Archangels are said to bring messages in the form of visions, occurrences, insights, deep perceptions, and mystical experiences, so that we can become more aware and rediscover our true beings. Printed on the Tablet of Jupiter are the numbers 1–16.

Apparently, sixteen is *the* number regarding the Tablet of Jupiter and I am assuming that Mrs. Le Breton has created *The White Magic Book* based on the wisdom she had derived from the Tablet. If you count the number of squares in her Table of Signs, you will see that there are sixteen of them. In each of the squares is one of either the seven above-mentioned planets of astrology or the nine above-mentioned signs of the zodiac (7 + 9 = 16).

I believe that her Tablet of Jupiter dates from the Middle Ages because, though Sumerian, Babylonian, and even later astrologers were well aware of all of the planets of our solar system, the seven planets used therein were the only planets visible to the naked eye until the invention of the telescope by the heroic Galileo. I cannot be sure where she found the Tablet, though Shakespeare does refer to a Tablet left by Jupiter in the play "Cymbeline." She may have just found it in an old book.

I must admit that I am also a little puzzled by Mrs. Le Breton's choice of the nine signs of the zodiac. In astrology, each sign is said to be "ruled" by a planet, which is another

The White Magic Book

way of saying that the qualities and energies exemplified by that planet in the language of astrology is most harmonious with those of a particular sign of the zodiac. In this case, the Sun ☉ is ruled by the sign Leo ♌, the Moon ☾ is ruled by Cancer ♋, Mars ♂ is ruled by Aries ♈, and Saturn ♄ is ruled by Capricorn ♑. However, in the days before the discovery of Uranus in 1781, Neptune in 1846, and Pluto in 1930, several of the seven visible planets used by Mrs. Le Breton were considered to rule more than one sign of the zodiac. Jupiter ♃, given prominence of place in the Table of Signs, was said to rule both Pisces ♓ and Sagittarius ♐, Venus was said to rule both Taurus ♉ and Libra ♎, and Mercury ☿ was said to rule both Virgo ♍ and Gemini ♊, but there is no Gemini in Mrs. Le Breton's Table of Signs! Aquarius and Scorpio are also missing. Why? It is a mystery.

And there are more of them. For instance, why has she started the pages of answers to the questions in the book with the page 5 and not page 1, as would be more conventional? I have a couple of educated guesses to decipher that one. Five is the number of points in a pentagram, the basic symbol of White Magic. A pentagram is always drawn inside a circle and the area within that circle is consecrated as a sacred space from which to make magic. Among the Greeks, the number five was a symbol of health and vitality. They taught that the five elements of reality are Earth, Fire, Air, Water, and Ether, which could easily be seen as their name for the subatomic particles that hold matter together. In astrology, the number 5 is associated with the fifth house of an astrological horoscope, the house of The Sun and the sign Leo. Each of the houses of astrology governs or has to do with the different mundane areas of our life. A planet passing through the fifth house of an astrological horoscope chart, either at the moment of our birth or anytime in our life, will trigger thoughts, issues, and events related to the creation of pleasurable things that have a life of their own. And, indeed, *The White Magic Book* and puzzles both could be considered pleasurable things that have a life of their own. Solving the puzzles of this book, to whatever degree, still leaves us with more puzzles to solve. It's like that with all good puzzles.

When I solve puzzles like this, I also—and I imagine you do to—experience the delightful feeling of having played a unique and valuable part in the universe's apparent game of getting to know itself better. One feels like one was in the right place at the right time. Though each and every minute of our lives is a gift filled with more magic than we can ever see, it is those rare moments of seemingly miraculous coincidence, accurate intuitions, and spontaneous insights that we treasure so, second only to our experience of love. In all these experiences, we feel connected to everything and whole in these moments of pure synchronicity.

The word synchronicity is derived from the Greek *syn* meaning "together" and *chronos* meaning "time." The theory of synchronicity, developed by the pioneering psychologist Carl Jung, postulates that things occurring at the same moment have a relationship of significance, if not of actual causality. This prescient theory predates Benoit Mandelbrot's chaos theory, which proves scientifically that a butterfly flapping its wings in Japan has a measurable and predictable effect on the weather in San Francisco.

From the founders of the world's religions to Albert Einstein's formula $E = MC^2$, and even many modern advertising campaigns, we have become aware that we are all con-

The White Magic Book

nected. This is, indeed, one of the scientific principles I wrote about earlier. However, nothing compares to the wonder and excitement of seeing this fact in action and actually experiencing synchronicity in one's life. There are as many ways to experience these "meaningful coincidences" as there are people in the world, yet some people see them as mere chance, while to others they are the living proof of the Great Spirit that animates all things.

Since the earliest days of humankind, it has been accepted without question that these moments of synchronicity and, especially, the people who are able to interpret and even predict special events are agents of the Divine. They are known as "oracles." Like the three-legged stool upon which sat the most famous of them all, the legendary Oracle of Apollo at Delphi, the word "oracle" has three meanings: the person who gives the pronouncement of the deity or divine force from whence the message comes; the shrine where the message is given; and finally, the message itself.

The White Magic Book is an oracle in all three senses of the word. The book is your personal, portable shrine, twenty-four-hour medium, the "person," and in it is the answer to your every question. All you have to do is use it with sincerity and an open mind and you will be truly surprised and delighted to experience moments of synchronicity on a daily basis.

Speaking of Synchronicity

It should not surprise anyone that the way Red Wheel came to reprint this timeless classic was as a result of such a moment. Its editor was searching through Donald Weiser's Alexandria Library-like antiquarian book room for a completely different kind of book. Something made her look under a large pile of

The White Magic Book

books. There it was! Even more astonishing, something made her want to open this book instead of one of the other great texts all around it. Having opened it, she couldn't help reading it—right then and there. It was as if this oracle had been silent long enough and had waited until the perfect moment to interact with its editor, and now, with you.

Turning for inspiration and guidance to an oracle like *The White Magic Book* is just like looking for information on the Internet. There's an almost infinite amount of it out there for you to access. But whatever information you find is going to help you only to the degree that you know how to interpret and make use of it.

This may or may not be a New Age but it is certainly what I like to call the Now Age. Everything seems to have to be done *now*. Too much information, too many things that have to be done now, and not enough time to do them, is making us all stressed-out nearly all the time. Gone is the cushion of time between communications that allowed you to thoughtfully consider the situation and your response to it. The very term "thoughtfully consider" seems to be a remnant of the distant past. We need to make use of the wisdom contained in *The White Magic Book*, not only because it was written when people thoughtfully considered things, but because using it regularly creates a ritual space in our lives where we can restore our connection with the quiet voice of our higher mind and benefit from its wise guidance. Creating this oasis of calm in the midst of the hectic pace of modern life is essential to our well-being.

When you select one of the book's ninety-five suggested questions, starting mysteriously not with question number 1 but question number 5, the act of melding your situation with

The White Magic Book

just the right question will almost immediately help you to clarify it somewhat. "If you know your question, you know your answer" is an old expression among those of us who use oracles every day.

The Ancient Art of Divination

I consult oracles every day, and I am proud to say that my wife, the artist Amy Zerner, and I are currently two of the world's most popular designers of personal oracles, also known as "divination systems" or "personal guidance systems." Since 1988, Amy and I have created our family of fourteen different divination systems based on a wide range of metaphysical subjects, including astrology, tarot cards, alchemy, psychic development, shamanism, affirmations, sacred love, and the Goddess. We have used each of them to help us conceive, create, manufacture, and market the next. There is no way in the world we could have become as successful as we have without them. We refer to them as our "spiritual power tools!"

The White Magic Book, is a pioneering work that serves to link Amy's and my work with the master oracles of old. It also helps you to connect with that same ancient wisdom. When you ask a question using *The White Magic Book*, you immediately join the long, unbroken line of questioners stretching back to the Oracle of Delphi and beyond.

An oracle is a sacred machine that can capture the holographic totality of information present in each and every moment and reflect it back to you for your consideration. The ancients used all manner of divination methods, many of which, to us, in our age of plastic-wrapped meats, seem unnecessarily bloody, such as examining the entrails of freshly killed animals. But the ancients could and did examine the way the

The White Magic Book

clouds or a flock of birds were looking or moving, or the way the wind was moving through the leaves or over the water, or the picture that formed in the bottom of a teacup or a crystal ball, or in the mind of a seer who stared into a mirror or flame. We can do all of those and more. The answers are all around us, if we will only take the time to stop, look, and listen.

Using an oracle was, and still is, considered a wise decision by the rich and powerful. In ancient times, rulers made long and arduous pilgrimages to put their questions to the living oracles of their time and region. Today, a symbol of our democratic times is the fact that it is no longer just the prerogative of the rich and powerful to consult a living oracle like a psychic, tarot reader, astrologer, medical intuitive, or other individual with a highly developed metaphysical ability. Each of us can do it all of the time.

However, any oracle worth his or her salt will always tell you that you, too, have the ability to read the signs around you, if you will only take the time to develop your intuition. The good news is that in addition to answering your question, *The White Magic Book*, when used correctly, with sincerity and pure intention, imparts the very valuable side benefit of sharpening your intuition. At its heart, *The White Magic Book* is a wonderful system for obtaining answers to almost every question you can think of.

I do wish I knew more about Mrs. John Le Breton, another puzzle for me to solve some day. But I do want to say I like the fact that the original language of her work has been preserved. This might seem puzzling to you after reading my strong feelings about the inequality of the sexes in this time of our emergence from the Dark Ages. The reason I believe it is appropriate to retain these obviously chauvinistic questions

The White Magic Book

and answers is that it is important for us to remember our place in time. It is crucial to do so when we're asking a question about the future. Remember the meaning of synchronicity: together in time.

Remember, too, we are all smart enough to be able to rephrase in our mind Mrs. Le Breton's suggested questions and answers for our purposes. When we do so let us give thanks for how far we have come and rededicate ourselves to further reducing the level of ignorance in the world. When she talks of "letters," let us realize that we have to include all methods of communication, like e-mail, phone calls, faxes, wireless devices, pagers, and greeting cards and letters, too. Think of how she would have been amazed to see the developments in communications that have come into being since her passing. When she talks about questions about longing and courting and marrying and being a husband or wife, give thanks for how much better things have become since the plight of the women of her time and how far they still have to go. But also think about the kernels of caring and the longing for genuine human connection that haven't changed and can be found in her questions and answers.

As a fellow designer of divination systems I have learned a lot about Mrs. John LeBaron from using and analyzing her work. She was knowledgeable, thorough, dedicated, original, and yet respectful of the traditions from which she drew her information, traditions that also offered wisdom for daily living. Her system answers my questions as promised. I only hope that people will say the same thing about Amy and me in 2101!

So—give it a try. Pick a question that is important to you at this very moment. Let the magic begin!

The White Magic Book

To us, the people of the twentieth century, the conquest of the air, the transmission of messages by wireless telegraphy, the harnessing of the terrific forces of electricity to our daily needs are sober facts of our everyday existence, exciting no wonderment and certainly no incredulity. It is a matter of common knowledge now that the skeleton of a living man can be photographed; and for a very small sum it is possible to purchase that amazing device which speaks and sings—perhaps with the voice of one now silenced for ever—or crashes out in the majestic harmony of a great orchestra in which almost every instrument can be identified. Yet, well within our memory these things would have been considered the wildest of impossibilities; and a little farther back down the dim vista of years, they would have been starkly denounced as—Magic.

And that is an absolutely correct definition, for what is Magic but phenomena resulting from the forces of Mind and Will—exactly and precisely the agencies though which these latter-day miracles have been achieved.

The Magi were the wise men of the East, the learned class, who devoted themselves to the study of Magic. They were the priests and politicians, and it was all to their interest to keep their discoveries secret and to invest them with mystery, for so they were able to retain supreme power in their

The White Magic Book

own hands and to awe the uninstructed masses. They ruled through a weak monarch, and aided a strong one. Pharaoh matched them against Aaron when Moses was making his oft-repeated demands for the release of a nation from slavery.

"And Aaron cast down his rod before Pharaoh, and before his servants, and it became a serpent.

Then Pharaoh also called the wise men and the sorcerers: now the magicians of Egypt, they also did in like manner with their enchantments.

"For they cast down every man his rod, and they became serpents."—*Exod.* vii. 10, 11, 12.

There came a period when Magic fell into disrepute, and many learned men and brilliant inventors suffered the death penalty for being in advance of their time— falling victims, together with innocent and ignorant people, unjustly accused by those who claimed to know what was possible and what was impossible.

Still later on, came the time when Magic was not even considered worthy of serious condemnation. Laughter and cheap sneers were a far more deadly treatment—the contempt of the "sensible" people who set themselves up as judges of what man can do, and what he can never accomplish.

De Balzac wrote of his time:

"It is the word 'absurd' which condemned steam, which condemns to-day aerial navigation, which condemned the inventions of gunpowder, of printing, of spectacles, of engineering, and the more recent art of photography. . . ." —*Comédie Humaine.*

Yet, some nineteen hundred odd years ago the Magi, or magicians, were held in reverence. To this day, the story of their coming to Jerusalem with their offering of gold and of

The White Magic Book

frankincense and myrrh is read in our place of public worship; and in the Scriptures no doubt or slur is cast upon their divination of the birth of the Messiah.

A dictionary, chosen because of its general use rather than for any especial merit, is consistently severe in its definitions of Magic and all allied terms until the word supernatural comes under notice—when it concedes practically everything which it has previously denied. Thus:

Magic (L. *Magicus,* from Magi): the *pretended* art of bringing into action the agency of supernatural beings.

Theurgy (Gr. *Theos,* God, and *ergon,* work): the *pretended* art of magic.

Psychomancy (Gr. *psyche,* the soul, and *manteia,* divination): necromancy, divination.

Necromancy (Gr. *nekros,* dead, and *manteia,* divination): divination by means of *pretended* communication with the dead; spirit-rapping; magic.

Necromancy is the ancient term for the modem cult of spiritism. Divination, the foretelling of future events or the discovery of things secret or obscure by *alleged* converse with supernatural powers.

Then comes the really essential word.

Supernatural, being beyond, or exceeding the known powers of Nature.

Mark that—"exceeding the *known* powers of Nature." Therefore, it may be reasonably claimed that what was supernatural even thirty years ago, i.e. beyond or exceeding the *known* powers of Nature, is no longer supernatural at the present time. Indeed, it is an undeniable fact. And what is today regarded as sheer folly (or supernatural) by the possessors of "plain common sense," may, in the not far distant future, rank as positive science.

Our dictionary does, however, admit psychology to be a science—the science of mind on the data of consciousness. And what is Mind? Never was a term so mis-used, so little understood. One is informed with authority that Mind is the thinking faculty, the spiritual principle or the soul in man: intention, purpose, inclination, desire, thought, opinion, memory. remembrance, disposition. It is also something else of far more importance.

Mind is your consciousness. It is *you*.

Immediately you grasp the idea, you will realise that it is the unassailable and simple truth—for only the very primitive human being imagines that his body is himself. Even in early childhood most of us are aware that we inhabit our bodies, and that they are the instruments of our wills and desires.

Man had to learn to develop his hand—so as to oppose the fingers singly or all together to the thumb. Thus was formed the perfect organ which gave him sovereignty of the earth. And man will have to learn to develop his Mind, which will give him powers that only a very few, scattered here and there among the teeming millions of humanity, have even begun to suspect.

Darwin, in his world-famous *Origin of Species*, made only one reference to psychology, and then in these few words, pregnant with meaning:

"In the future, I see open fields for far more important researches. Psychology will be securely based on the foundation already well laid by Mr. Herbert Spencer, that of the necessary acquirement of each mental power and capacity by gradation."

The White Magic Book

'The necessary acquirement of each mental power and capacity by gradation." That prediction was first published on November 24th, 1859—yet the students of psychology are still numbered only by hundreds. We are even now living in the Dark Ages.

Mind is your consciousness. Mind is *you*. But you are part of the Universal Consciousness, the Universal Mind, by which and in which we live. The distinguished French scientist, M. Goupil, writing to a no less famous French astronomer, has put it very clearly.

"Take a handful of the ocean, and you have *water*.

Take a handful of the atmosphere, and you have *air*.

Take a handful of space, and you have *Mind*.

That is the way I interpret it. That is why Mind is always present, ready to respond when it finds in any place a stimulus that incites it, and an organism which permits it to manifest itself."

How can you develop your Mind—how can you learn to use the power which is latent in every normal human being?

Rely upon yourself and learn to use your judgment in every detail of your daily life. You have free will and freedom of choice, and if you do not exercise them the responsibility is yours—and it is one which cannot be evaded. Realise the power of your Mind, however little it is, and begin to use it consciously and firmly without a minute's delay. The power of your Mind is as real and actual a force as the power of your hand. That which your mind pictures clearly, and your will demands strongly and untiringly, you can draw to you and make your own, sooner or later. No argument is necessary to convince you of the accuracy of this statement, for you can see it working out continually and exactly around you as you go through life.

The White Magic Book

You wonder why so many people suffer from poverty? Look about you at the poor whom you may happen to know personally. Do they steadily and continuously demand prosperity, make the image of it in their minds, keep on the alert for the coming of it, and plan out the way in which it shall come? No! the people who have done these things and are doing them, *are* prosperous, and will become more so. They are using their Minds, though perhaps unconsciously. Those who suffer from poverty do so because:

They take what is given to them, and seek for nothing better.

They complain of their hard fate, and settle down to endure it.

They convince themselves that poverty is their lot, and that finishes the matter so far as they are concerned.

Many a friendless, uneducated, delicate, penniless boy has before now risen not only to immense wealth, but to fame, by sheer force of will and power of Mind. Such object-lessons are in themselves sufficient proof of what can be done—unaided—by those who resolve to use their natural forces and persevere in doing so.

Everything that man has made for his use, comfort, convenience or pleasure has existed in thought before it became a reality. Someone made a mental picture of the conveyance which you travel in, of the home you live in, of the pen you write with, even of the very clothes you wear before they could become realities. The will-power of someone was brought to bear upon those thought-pictures, and they developed into actualities.

You can do the same if you still be determined and persistent.

The White Magic Book

Was there ever a stronger or more ceaseless demand than that of mankind for the power to fly? Was there ever an aspiration more pitilessly derided and scoffed at? Yet the demand has been met, and a lad at play in the air, looping the loop or driving at breathless speed among the sunset clouds attracts no more attention than one who takes his pleasures among the waves of the sea, as his ancestors have done before him century after century.

Man is a much more wonderful and complex creation than he supposed himself to be even a few years ago. *You* are much more wonderful than perhaps you imagine yourself to be, at present. You can understand and realise your five senses. Try to realise the power of your Mind.

That great investigator of psychic phenomena, Myers, writes in *The Human Personality:* "Medical observation (Félida, Alma) proves that there is in us a rudimentary supernormal faculty, something which is probably useless to us, but which indicates the existence, beneath the level of our consciousness, of a reserve of latent unsuspected faculties."

A reserve of latent unsuspected *faculties*—a reserve of latent powers of *Mind*.

Even an animal can bring its mind-force to bear on sensitive people. Who has not seen a dog intent on watching its owner, silent and motionless, yet obsessed with one idea which positively radiates from it, and which sooner or later will make itself felt by the person to whom it is directed. Perhaps the dog wants to be taken out for exercise, or it needs food or drink—or caresses. There is no doubt that it conceives an idea, makes a mental picture of what it so strongly desires, and then settles down to put into action that force which all living creatures possess in a greater or lesser degree. To my own knowledge, horses developed mentally by human companionship and affection are capable of making similar communications and from a considerable distance.

"The universe is a great organism controlled by a dynamism of the psychical order. Mind gleams through its every atom. The environment or atmosphere is psychic. There is Mind in everything, not only in human and animal life, but in plants, in minerals, in space."—*Mysterious Psychic Forces:* Camille Flammarion.

Everything that man needs for his happiness and wellbeing is within his reach, and his "latent unsuspected faculties" when developed and brought into constant use will make him more consciously master of his fate than he is now.

Realise your Mind—realise your consciousness. Then, choose wisely, concentrate your Mind steadily and strongly upon what you have chosen until you have made it your own.

To concentrate is simply to steady the Mind to its use, just as a skilled workman would steady his hand for work.

Wealth being the means of purchasing practically everything for the ease of body and gratification of the senses, the mass of people make that the first demand. It is a truism that "wealth does not always bring happiness." Those who concentrate upon the idea of wealth to the exclusion of all else, generally attain it—and prove the saying. I could instance hoarding peasants to whom a hundred or a couple of hundred pounds represented wealth, and who, fixing that sum as a limit, secured it through incredible exertions and deprivations—losing priceless health and domestic happiness by the way; and successful business men, desolate amidst their opulence at the end of a strenuous career—because everything had dropped away from them excepting the wealth which cannot buy youth or health or love—or peace.

The White Magic Book

Therefore, use your judgment and choose wisely when you bring your power of Mind into action. Be very sure that what you desire will be for your benefit—because if you are sincere and strong and persistent in using this great natural force of yours, you will most certainly draw to yourself exactly what you have imagined and that which you have resolved to acquire.

One fact, accurately and dispassionately observed, is worth countless arguments. There is only one satisfactory way to acquire knowledge, and that is to investigate for oneself. Here is such a fact.

A clever and popular actress, well known to London audiences at one time, was in due course obliged to yield to the younger generation, but as a member of No. 1 touring companies continued to enjoy success, and incidentally to see a great deal of the world; but when a touring company's way lies through English provinces, life is not strewn with roses and a continuous endurance of minor discomforts and petty hardships inevitably produced a condition of profound discontent. A peculiarly atrocious experience in "apartments" brought matters to a climax. Although a woman of hot temper and quick and vivid emotions, she possessed much self-control, but—quite suddenly—she broke down and wept with sheer rage and resentment against fate. It was over in a moment, but the impression left was ineffaceable. "If I only had a *home*," she said, locking her hands together, and speaking with tremendous intensity, "anything—*anything* but this ghastly wandering from one hideous lodging to another. Just a *home!*"

She had formed a mind-picture, it was her nature to hold it tenaciously, and she did so. A few months later, by what was then described to me as "mere chance," she came into contact with a philanthropist who was at the time establishing the first of his homes for the benefit of ladies with extremely small independent means—and through him, her demand was met generously—splendidly. She left the stage and she had a home. It was a mansion, fitted with every modern convenience, luxuriously, even beautifully furnished, well-staffed, well-served in every way. The great-hearted founder was a millionaire, and while he lived it was his chief pleasure to ensure the happiness of those whom he had taken under his care—as much so as though they had been members of his own family. He died, and the management of affairs passed into the hands of trustees whose principal occupation became the making of rules. One rule was to the effect that ladies should not leave the home even to visit friends, excepting for a stipulated number of weeks each year, *under any circumstances whatever.*

It was exactly what my friend had demanded—the antithesis of her former mode of existence; it was also a gilded prison from which, after some years of endurance, she freed herself, very gladly. To her, at least, the sequence of events needs no explanation.

To quote the celebrated French astronomer Camille Flammarion again:

"At the basis of all is force, dynamism, and universal Mind or spirit.

"Your heart beats night and day, whatever be the position of your body. The embryo is formed in the womb of the mother, in the egg of the bird. There is neither heart nor brain.

"At a certain moment the heart beats for the first time. Sublime moment! . . . Who or what wound up this watch once for all?

The White Magic Book

"Dynamism, the vital energy.

"What sustains the earth in space?

"Dynamism, the velocity of its movement.

"What is it in the bullet that kills?

"Its velocity.

"Everywhere energy, everywhere the invisible element."

Every one of your thoughts is a part of this vital energy, and it is your duty to yourself and to humanity to develop your force and to use it.

Admitted that this force exists—how can we use it?

First and foremost, acquire the art of self-control. Learn to control your will, your Mind-force, your emotions. Anger creates an actual poison in the blood—people have died of fear. To each, is their own special failing, and quiet consideration will inform you better on this point than any advice which can be offered.

But, above all, self-control. Lightning destroys. Controlled electricity has conferred countless benefits upon humanity.

A medical man is said to have a "bedside manner." What does it mean? Perfect self-control, combined with helpful suggestion. Mind-power consciously and skillfully used for the purpose of healing. A doctor subject to variations of temper during the exercise of his profession would be not only useless, but actually harmful.

A wave of intense interest in psychical research is sweeping over the world, and on the outskirts of the crowd of earnest enquirers, hangs the inevitable fringe of those who take it up as a mode, a fashion, something to enhance the interest of their personality. Remember that there are frauds in every walk of life, and some of them deceive themselves. Do not be discouraged by the man whose talk is all of

The White Magic Book

occultism, and who a moment later exhibits signs of intense annoyance or perhaps depression over some untoward occurrence. Or the woman who will paint her face to simulate the bloom of health, and draw your attention to it with the unnecessary explanation, "What I am, I have made myself." Such as these there have always been, and "by their works ye shall know them."

Be sincere, be self-controlled, be persevering. Choose wisely. Concentrate your Mind-power steadily and strongly upon your desire. Demand, and you will receive.

To the power of Mind may be attributed the extraordinary phenomena produced by "mediums" who profess to be in touch with the spirit world. The phenomena actually do occur, and those who are responsible for them are quite possibly unaware of the nature of their own powers. The levitation of tables without contact, for instance, has been proved beyond all doubt by the evidence of men of science whose names have a world-wide renown. But, on the Malabar coast, the home of Indian Magic, I have seen a magician—one who practised the "pretended" art of magic—stretch himself upon a cot brought out from the servant's quarters, and in broad daylight, by sheer Mind-force raise that cot four to six inches from the ground, so that a *lâthi* or stick could be passed freely under the legs of it. That was claimed to be Magic. There was no suggestion that a disembodied spirit had produced the phenomenon.

And other feats of Magic I have seen, also in full sunshine, much more wonderful.

However, the further one explores in the regions of psychic force, the more difficult it becomes to use the word "impossible." Therefore, with regard to Spiritism and all kindred subjects, it is well to remain open to conviction.

The White Magic Book

It is generally admitted—and deplored—that the most successful mediums are ill-educated, and sometimes illiterate. It would be indeed strange if departed spirits should deliberately elect to manifest themselves through such unworthy vehicles; but it is not at all strange that these people should be capable of exerting their Mind-forces to such an extraordinary degree. Having discovered their natural powers, they concentrate upon the development of them to the exclusion of all else, unhampered (and uncontrolled) by the influences of education. It is a fact that in highly-educated people Mind is sometimes impotent through non-use. The psychic force has been neglected until it is more feeble than that possessed by ignorant and possibly unscrupulous mediums. The Mind-power of the latter is a strong and untrained force, and therefore dangerous. That of the former is weak and untrained—practically useless in its present condition.

Until now, no text-book has been at the disposal of the vast and ever-increasing numbers of those who are eager to study the science of Mind, and who naturally wish to begin at the beginning.

The Book of White Magic claims only to rank as a primer, and as such it should be the first study of all who aware of immature and unused Mind-power. To place in the hands of such, the esoteric works of those great ones, the scientific pioneers of psychical research is as if one should invest a child with the prerogatives of manhood, and expect him to use them to his profit.

With regard to the method fully explained in the pages headed *"Table of Signs and How to Use It,"* the very simplicity of it is its strongest recommendation. There must be a method of arriving at any result, and if a simple one can be discovered,

The White Magic Book

so much the better. It is *only* the alphabet which is used in the composition of words; and those words which rank column after column in the emotionless pages of a dictionary are the very same words which a master-hand weaves into the magic and music of a deathless poem.

Before you are the lowest rungs of the ladder of knowledge of *yourself* and your wonderful powers; and even the first step is the beginning of an ascension from the depths to the heights.

Introduction

Choose a *suitable* question, and one to which you honestly desire an answer.

Concentrate all your thoughts on that question.

Mentally demand that the answer which you *need* shall come to you.

At the moment when you make the demand, close your eyes and touch the Table of Signs.

*   *   *   *   *

You may have selected Question 76.

And, on the Table of Signs, you may have touched the Symbol of Venus ♀. In that case—

Make a note of the number of your question.

Turn to the pages of figures.

Find the number of your question in the column on the extreme left.

Trace straight from it *toward the right* until you reach the column headed with ♀.

Here, you will find the number of the page on which is your answer—page 19.

On page 19, *opposite* the Symbol of Venus ♀, you will find the answer to your question.

Table of Signs and How to Use It

"Your careless thinking has little or no result—while your concrete thoughts have definite mathematical results."

That is what one of America's foremost thinkers has written and it is a truth which is being more and more widely accepted every day in the new world which is being evolved amidst the upheaval caused by the Great War.

Thought is a real force—and thought is the product of the mind; but the great masses of the people have never learned to use their minds, never trained them to concentrate upon what is needed or desired and so to draw it within reach.

A well-developed and well-balanced mind, directed by an active will-power should be able to concentrate upon a given subject and consider it for just so long as its owner chooses. And, how many people are capable of such a mental feat as that? Not one in a thousand—not one in ten thousand. The thoughts of the average man or woman flit from one subject to another with the careless rapidity of butterflies upon a day of summer sunshine.

In every normal human being, the will-power should be roused and the mind awakened to its possibilities; but this can only be done by degrees, just as physical strength is first realised in extreme youth and later on increased by use and deliberate intention.

The White Magic Book

Here is a fascinating mind-exercise—whether it is something more depends upon yourself.

Certain conditions are absolutely necessary to a successful issue. You must choose a *suitable* question and one to which you honestly desire an answer.

Concentrate all your thoughts on that question.

Mentally demand that the answer which you *need* shall come to you.

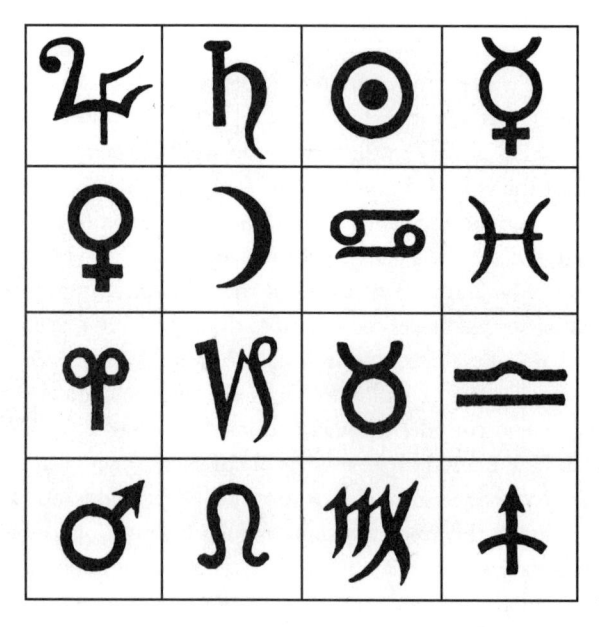

♃	♄	☉	☿
♀	☽	♋	♓
♈	♑	♉	♎
♂	♌	♍	♐

At the moment when you make the demand, close your eyes and touch the Table of Signs.

You may have selected Question 76. *"Shall I ever possess any property in my own right?"* And, on the Table of Signs, you *may* have touched the Symbol of Venus ♀.

The White Magic Book

In that case, having *noted down* the *number* of your question, turn to the fourth page of figures.

Find the number of your question (76) in the column on the extreme left.

Trace straight from it *toward the right* until you reach the column which is headed with ♀. There, you will find the number of the page on which is your answer—page 19.

On page 19, opposite the Symbol of Venus ♀, you will find the answer to your question.

But, if you should have touched any other sign, proceed in the same way, searching for *that* sign. *Your* sign will bring *your* answer to you.

The thing will be as you make it. Use in sincerity, and you will be amazed at the accuracy of the results. Be foolish over it, and you will be repaid in your own coin. Bring a carping humour to bear upon it, and ask, "*Shall I be married while I am young?*" when perhaps you are no longer young, and possibly are already married—and the Table of Signs will play you a queer little trick of making it impossible for you to get an answer at all—unless you persist again and again, and then what you get will be worthless to you.

If your demand is strong, and your mind is open to conviction, you will certainly draw the information which you require to you. Failure can only come by reason of insufficient strength or by the intentional folly of the user.

Tests have been made hundreds of times before publication, and in not one single instance has there been a failure to record.

Such is the explanation of the method, which is simple as all wonderful things are simple. It is left to you to experiment and to verify the results.

But, remember, that there is no such thing as Chance. Earth and the heavens and all that in them is, are governed by Law.

Questions

---

5. Shall I be engaged soon?
6. Does the one I am thinking about, think of me?
7. What is the reason of the estrangement between the man whom I like so much, and myself?
8. Will there be a change of residence for me before long?
9. Can I win the love that I desire?
10. Would it be wise to answer this letter?
11. What will happen if I keep my appointment?
12. Ought I to trust the woman who seems so anxious to be my friend?
13. Will my husband be young?
14. Shall I marry more than once?
15. Shall I ever completely regain my health?
16. What does the man whom I love, really think of me?
17. Will the visit that I am about to make, be a success?
18. Ought I to believe what . . . tells me?
19. Why does not my friend write to me?
20. Has anyone created ill feeling between . . . and myself?
21. Shall I marry while I am young?
22. Shall I have many adventures?
23. Will my husband make me happy?
24. Is . . . loyal to me?
25. Will the secret of my life remain a secret?
26. Will my husband let me have my own way?

The White Magic Book

27. Shall I have any children?
28. Shall I ever be rich?
29. Will my husband be jealous?
30. What do people think of me?
31. What are the distinguishing characteristics of my future wife?
32. What does the immediate future hold for me?
33. Will my friends be pleased to hear of my engagement?
34. Shall I marry . . . ?
35. How shall I recognise my future husband?
36. Ought I to carry out the plans which I have made?
37. Shall I ever have my heart's desire?
38. Shall I be happy in my love-affairs?
39. What have I to expect during the next twelve months?
40. Shall I marry where money is?
41. Of what disposition will my husband be?
42. What is the reason of . . . 's enmity toward me?
43. Will my husband be clever?
44. Have I any rivals?
45. Shall I ever be involved in any legal proceedings?
46. Shall I be fortunate in business?
47. Does the future hold any special danger for me?
48. Have I already met my future life-partner?
49. Will our disagreement last long?
50. Will the reconciliation be favourable to me?
51. Am I loved as much as when I was first engaged?
52. Shall I ever become well-known?
53. Shall I ever make the acquaintance of the person who attracts me so much?
54. Will . . . return soon?
55. Does . . . always tell me the truth?

The White Magic Book

56. Will my present worries last long?
57. When shall I receive the news which I am expecting?
58. When will the affair in which I am interested end?
59. Which of the two persons of whom I am thinking values my friendship the more?
60. When shall I receive the gift which I am expecting?
61. Shall I have many long voyages?
62. Ought I to continue to live under the same roof with . . . ?
63. Will my position soon be changed?
64. What will be the result of my present anxieties?
65. I wish! Will my wish be fulfilled?
66. Ought I to forgive . . . ?
67. Is . . . really sorry for what has happened?
68. Ought I to tell . . . everything?
69. Ought I to take the first step toward a reconciliation?
70. Ought I to oppose my husband's plans for the future?
71. Will . . . give me full explanation?
72. Is there sorrow in store for me?
73. Have I to expect loss of money?
74. What is . . . thinking about at this moment?
75. Is anyone envious of me?
76. Shall I ever possess any property in my own right?
77. Should I be more successful in my native land, or abroad?
78. Will there be any scandal talked about me?
79. How will the world use me?
80. Is my occupation the one in which I am most likely to make a success?
81. What has become of the thing which I have lost?
82. Will my life be a peaceful one?

The White Magic Book

83. Ought I to live in the country or in a town?
84. Is there any foundation for the fear that I have at times?
85. Born between the 91st and 120th days of the year, what have I especially to guard against?
86. Shall I ever discover the truth about...?
87. Are my suspicions about ... correct?
88. What profession or business will my husband follow?
89. Born between the 32nd and 59th days of the year, what will guide me to happiness?
90. Born in the seventh month of the year, which of my characteristics will most strongly influence my future?
91. Born between the 60th and 90th days of the year, what must I do to ensure good fortune?
92. Born in the eighth month of the year, what dates are the most fortunate for me?
93. Will my old age be prosperous and happy?
94. How can I make my future successful?
95. Have I enemies?
96. How shall I recognise my enemy?
97. Shall I ever have a home of my own?
98. Will my home be all that I wish?
99. Shall I ever escape from the sadness which overshadows me at times?
100. Will my powers of memory ever improve?

The White Magic Book

Signs Corresponding to the Answers on Each Page

Number of Question	♃	♄	☉	☿	♀	☽	♋	♓	♈	♑	♉	♎	♂	♌	♏	✝
5	20	26	32	38	44	50	56	62	68	74	80	86	92	98	8	14
6	21	27	33	39	45	51	57	63	69	75	81	87	93	99	9	15
7	22	28	34	40	46	52	58	64	70	76	82	88	94	100	10	16
8	23	29	35	41	47	53	59	65	71	77	83	89	95	5	11	17
9	24	30	36	42	48	54	60	66	72	78	84	90	96	6	12	18
10	25	31	37	43	49	55	61	67	73	79	85	91	97	7	13	19
11	26	32	38	44	50	56	62	68	74	80	86	92	98	8	14	20
12	27	33	39	45	51	57	63	69	75	81	87	93	99	9	15	21
13	28	34	40	46	52	58	64	70	76	82	88	94	100	10	16	22
14	29	35	41	47	53	59	65	71	77	83	89	95	5	11	17	23
15	30	36	42	48	54	60	66	72	78	84	90	96	6	12	18	24
16	31	37	43	49	55	61	67	73	79	85	91	97	7	13	19	25
17	32	38	44	50	56	62	68	74	80	86	92	98	8	14	20	26
18	33	39	45	51	57	63	69	75	81	87	93	99	9	15	21	27
19	34	40	46	52	58	64	70	76	82	88	94	100	10	16	22	28
20	35	41	47	53	59	65	71	77	83	89	95	5	11	17	23	29
21	36	42	48	54	60	66	72	78	84	90	96	6	12	18	24	30
22	37	43	49	55	61	67	73	79	85	91	97	7	13	19	25	31
23	38	44	50	56	62	68	74	80	86	92	98	8	14	20	26	32

xliii

The White Magic Book

Signs Corresponding to the Answers on Each Page

Number of Question	♃	♄	☉	☿	♀	☽	♋	♓	⚷	♈	♉	♎	♂	♌	♍	†
24	39	45	51	57	63	69	75	81	87	93	99	9	15	21	27	33
25	40	46	52	58	64	70	76	82	88	94	100	10	16	22	28	34
26	41	47	53	59	65	71	77	83	89	95	5	11	17	23	29	35
27	42	48	54	60	66	72	78	84	90	96	6	12	18	24	30	36
28	43	49	55	61	67	73	79	85	91	97	7	13	19	25	31	37
29	44	50	56	62	68	74	80	86	92	98	8	14	20	26	32	38
30	45	51	57	63	69	75	81	87	93	99	9	15	21	27	33	39
31	46	52	58	64	70	76	82	88	94	100	10	16	22	28	34	40
32	47	53	59	65	71	77	83	89	95	5	11	17	23	29	35	41
33	48	54	60	66	72	78	84	90	96	6	12	18	24	30	36	42
34	49	55	61	67	73	79	85	91	97	7	13	19	25	31	37	43
35	50	56	62	68	74	80	86	92	98	8	14	20	26	32	38	44
36	51	57	63	69	75	81	87	93	99	9	15	21	27	33	39	45
37	52	58	64	70	76	82	88	94	100	10	16	22	28	34	40	46
38	53	59	65	71	77	83	89	95	5	11	17	23	29	35	41	47
39	54	60	66	72	78	84	90	96	6	12	18	24	30	36	42	48
40	55	61	67	73	79	85	91	97	7	13	19	25	31	37	43	49
41	56	62	68	74	80	86	92	98	8	14	20	26	32	38	44	50
42	57	63	69	75	81	87	93	99	9	15	21	27	33	39	45	51
43	58	64	70	76	82	88	94	100	10	16	22	28	34	40	46	52

The White Magic Book

Signs Corresponding to the Answers on Each Page

Number of Question	♃	♄	☉	☿	♀	☽	♋	♓	♅	♑	♉	♎	♂	♌	♍	♆
44	59	65	71	77	83	89	95	5	11	17	23	29	35	41	47	53
45	60	66	72	78	84	90	96	6	12	18	24	30	36	42	48	54
46	61	67	73	79	85	91	97	7	13	19	25	31	37	43	49	55
47	62	68	74	80	86	92	98	8	14	20	26	32	38	44	50	56
48	63	69	75	81	87	93	99	9	15	21	27	33	39	45	51	57
49	64	70	76	82	88	94	100	10	16	22	28	34	40	46	52	58
50	65	71	77	83	89	95	5	11	17	23	29	35	41	47	53	59
51	66	72	78	84	90	96	6	12	18	24	30	36	42	48	54	60
52	67	73	79	85	91	97	7	13	19	25	31	37	43	49	55	61
53	68	74	80	86	92	98	8	14	20	26	32	38	44	50	56	62
54	69	75	81	87	93	99	9	15	21	27	33	39	45	51	57	63
55	70	76	82	88	94	100	10	16	22	28	34	40	46	52	58	64
56	71	77	83	89	95	5	11	17	23	29	35	41	47	53	59	65
57	72	78	84	90	96	6	12	18	24	30	36	42	48	54	60	66
58	73	79	85	91	97	7	13	19	25	31	37	43	49	55	61	67
59	74	80	86	92	98	8	14	20	26	32	38	44	50	56	62	68
60	75	81	87	93	99	9	15	21	27	33	39	45	51	57	63	69
61	76	82	88	94	100	10	16	22	28	34	40	46	52	58	64	70
62	77	83	89	95	5	11	17	23	29	35	41	47	53	59	65	71

The White Magic Book

Signs Corresponding to the Answers on Each Page

Number of Question	♃	♄	☉	☿	♀	☽	♋	♓	☊	♑	♉	♎	♂	♌	♍	♐
63	78	84	90	96	6	12	18	24	30	36	42	48	54	60	66	72
64	79	85	91	97	7	13	19	25	31	37	43	49	55	61	67	73
65	80	86	92	98	8	14	20	26	32	38	44	50	56	62	68	74
66	81	87	93	99	9	15	21	27	33	39	45	51	57	63	69	75
67	82	88	94	100	10	16	22	28	34	40	46	52	58	64	70	76
68	83	89	95	5	11	17	23	29	35	41	47	53	59	65	71	77
69	84	90	96	6	12	18	24	30	36	42	48	54	60	66	72	78
70	85	91	97	7	13	19	25	31	37	43	49	55	61	67	73	79
71	86	92	98	8	14	20	26	32	38	44	50	56	62	68	74	80
72	87	93	99	9	15	21	27	33	39	45	51	57	63	69	75	81
73	88	94	100	10	16	22	28	34	40	46	52	58	64	70	76	82
74	89	95	5	11	17	23	29	35	41	47	53	59	65	71	77	83
75	90	96	6	12	18	24	30	36	42	48	54	60	66	72	78	84
76	91	97	7	13	19	25	31	37	43	49	55	61	67	73	79	85
77	92	98	8	14	20	26	32	38	44	50	56	62	68	74	80	86
78	93	99	9	15	21	27	33	39	45	51	57	63	69	75	81	87
79	94	100	10	16	22	28	34	40	46	52	58	64	70	76	82	88
80	95	5	11	17	23	29	35	41	47	53	59	65	71	77	83	89
81	96	6	12	18	24	30	36	42	48	54	60	66	72	78	84	90

The White Magic Book

Signs Corresponding to the Answers on Each Page

Number of Question	♃	♄	☉	☿	♀	☽	♋	♓	♆	♎	♉	♌	♂	♌	♍	♄
82	97	7	13	19	25	31	37	43	49	55	61	67	73	79	85	91
83	98	8	14	20	26	32	38	44	50	56	62	68	74	80	86	92
84	99	9	15	21	27	33	39	45	51	57	63	69	75	81	87	93
85	100	10	16	22	28	34	40	46	52	58	64	70	76	82	88	94
86	5	11	17	23	29	35	41	47	53	59	65	71	77	83	89	95
87	6	12	18	24	30	36	42	48	54	60	66	72	78	84	90	96
88	7	13	19	25	31	37	43	49	55	61	67	73	79	85	91	97
89	8	14	20	26	32	38	44	50	56	62	68	74	80	86	92	98
90	9	15	21	27	33	39	45	51	57	63	69	75	81	87	93	99
91	10	16	22	28	34	40	46	52	58	64	70	76	82	88	94	100
92	11	17	23	29	35	41	47	53	59	65	71	77	83	89	95	5
93	12	18	24	30	36	42	48	54	60	66	72	78	84	90	96	6
94	13	19	25	31	37	43	49	55	61	67	73	79	85	91	97	7
95	14	20	26	32	38	44	50	56	62	68	74	80	86	92	98	8
96	15	21	27	33	39	45	51	57	63	69	75	81	87	93	99	9
97	16	22	28	34	40	46	52	58	64	70	76	82	88	94	100	10
98	17	23	29	35	41	47	53	59	65	71	77	83	89	95	5	11
99	18	24	30	36	42	48	54	60	66	72	78	84	90	96	6	12
100	19	25	31	37	43	49	55	61	67	73	79	85	91	97	7	13

The White Magic Book

♃	A woman will enlighten you—quite unconsciously.
♄	You should have been a healer, mental and physical.
☉	Wishing to be with you.
☿	Be frank. It is the best way.
♀	No.
☽	Before the end of the month an improvement will set in.
♋	It would be a misfortune for you, in either case.
♓	One, who in other respects is your friend.
♈	There will be more pain than pleasure.
♑	Something that will please you much.
♉	Sometimes. Not often.
♎	Some people enjoy having a little grievance. Don't worry over it.
♂	You will refuse to do so.
♌	Someone bars the way. Possibly, it is yourself.
♍	It will be your stronghold against the world.
♐	Two hundred and seventy-second; and three hundred and twenty-seventh days of the year.

The White Magic Book

♃	Very nearly so.
♄	There is just a possibility that it may be restored to you.
☉	Yes, because you are what you are.
☿	If you do so once, you will be given many opportunities of doing so again.
♀	Yes, if you act cautiously and cleverly *now*.
☾	When you least look for it.
♋	You have had your share of romance. Be satisfied with what comes afterward.
♓	You will not be one of the principals in the affair.
♈	Some loss and some gain.
♑	They will consider that you are very fortunate.
♉	Yes, when you have found what you have not now.
♎	The time should be now.
♂	You need have no fear on that point.
♌	It is yours; but there are reasons why the matter may go no further.
♍	Within fourteen months, the world will seem a much better place to you.
♐	Yes, as you will thoroughly deserve.

The White Magic Book

♃	A pleasant, but not a very lucrative one.
♄	Not altogether, but peace will predominate.
☉	Through your own exertions—in no other way.
☿	Urge a further consideration—it is very necessary.
♀	There will be none.
☽	Serious difficulties cause the delay.
♋	Among a large circle of friends, no more.
♓	There are obstacles, but they only mean delay.
♈	There will be periods of great prosperity.
♑	It will mean happiness for both if you do.
♉	Fairly; but there will be hard times first.
♎	None, if you are wise.
♂	That you look for pleasure first, last, and all the while.
♌	Answer it when you may, it will be too soon.
♍	Before very long you will notice a marked improvement; but keep even-tempered.
♐	By exercising some restraint over your fancy for free speech.

The White Magic Book

♃	Be just a little more cautious, especially in money-matters.
♄	To live in the country you would need a more well-balanced mind than you have at present.
☉	In the West of the world.
☿	Not unless you insist.
♀	Do not count upon it.
☽	The one to whom you have given your confidence.
♋	You would soon be disenchanted—if you kept your wits about you.
♓	Keep away from crowds or you will regret it.
♈	Excellent in manner, intelligent and hardworking.
♑	Medium height. Comes from overseas. Has a strange accent.
♉	No. He is prepared to manage you.
♎	Yes, if you are reasonable.
♂	It will not be roses all the way.
♌	That it will be followed by many more.
♍	No.
♐	Only those who fear that you may leave them behind in the race of life.

The White Magic Book

♃	Your sympathetic nature which will make you much beloved.
♄	There is no danger but in your own thoughts.
☉	Perhaps for some time, but not for ever.
☿	You need not think of it yet. It is very far away.
♀	Yes; but do not forget.
☽	You will lose nothing by the waiting.
♋	Already on the way, but it is a long road.
♓	You have seen each other.
♈	Your natural gifts.
♑	The result will not give you complete satisfaction—if any.
♉	Very proud, and with some reason to be so.
♎	Exactly as much so as you are.
♂	Absolutely.
♌	She is not so anxious as you think to obtain it.
♍	Thinks and also talks.
♐	Is treacherous, selfish, and very fond of good living.

The White Magic Book

♃	Do not anticipate failure. That is your weak point.
♄	Nervous illness. Be very careful of your general health.
☉	Not at all. You have always despised it, and always will.
☿	Yes; but not over the matter which you are considering at present.
♀	Much trouble has been taken to make you think so.
☽	Several journeys by land and by sea.
♋	No, fortunately for you.
♓	If it finishes tonight, it will begin again tomorrow.
♈	Not so much so as yourself.
♑	It is yours if you know how to wait.
♉	She will be a good friend and an unrelenting enemy.
♎	Continue to be discreet and there is nothing to fear.
♂	Pressed for time and considerably worried.
♌	He looks much younger than he is.
♍	He does not like those who are around you.
♐	Yes, much sooner than you imagine.

The White Magic Book

♃	January 5th, April 7th and 20th.
♄	Yes, quite by accident.
☉	You are not using your exceptional powers of organisation.
☿	Of an interesting conversation which is now taking place.
♀	You have not the courage to do so.
☽	Not if you can see your way to another arrangement.
♋	Half the time that they have already lasted.
♓	Very much so if you are careful.
♈	Yes.
♑	They will always make Paradise for you.
♉	One invitation, perhaps more.
♎	Practically never.
♂	No. Such an exacting nature can never be satisfied.
♌	You will not have the opportunity.
♍	Within sixteen months.
♐	You will envy no one after you have been in it a few days.

The White Magic Book

♃	More so than you will have really deserved.
♄	You are not altogether mistaken.
☉	It is not lost.
☿	No one on whom you need waste a thought.
♀	Let the other side make the approach.
☽	If you change it yourself. Not otherwise.
♋	Not until your patience has been severely tried.
♓	Keep good-humoured and you will not need to ask.
♈	It is extremely likely.
♑	An offer which you would do well to accept.
♉	Some of them will be jealous.
♎	Sooner or later.
♂	You must come out of that blind alley first, and the sooner the better.
♌	You *know* that you are recovering. Keep the fact always in mind.
♍	You lack opportunities. Given those, you would soon have your wish.
♐	Yes, because you will presently realise that you must make the *best* of life for the sake of others.

The White Magic Book

♃	Make your plans slowly and carry them out promptly.
♄	A money-making business.
☉	You will not allow it to be so.
☿	Yes. It will come to you from the earth.
♀	Not if you are independent. Otherwise, yes.
☽	Not the one which you fear.
♋	There are many and great difficulties to be overcome yet.
♓	Yes, in a neighbourhood.
♈	You have but to stretch out your hand to grasp success.
♑	Enough for complete comfort.
♉	It is not impossible yet, whatever some people may think.
♎	Yes—through no merit of your own.
♂	Yes, in a far country.
☊	That you are inclined to be exacting.
♍	If you do, remember that more than one person will see it.
♐	Do not allow anything or anyone to annoy you, and there need be no more anxiety on that score.

The White Magic Book

♃	There are people about you who need watching.
♄	Remember that even the most attractive people are not so straightforward as you are yourself.
☉	You will be happier in town even if not so healthy.
☿	Here, but further North.
♀	A good deal of discretion will be exercised.
☽	Your own action will direct the course of events.
♋	The one who acts, not merely talks.
♓	Don't do anything unusual—that person would strongly disapprove.
♈	Nothing but what your alert mind will protect you from.
♑	Likes to hear his own voice. Inclined to be very obstinate.
♉	Rather sunburned. Sturdily built. Very fine features.
♎	You will never be allowed to know it, if he is.
♂	Yes, by letting you make him happy.
♌	On the contrary, a little disappointing.
♍	That you will gain a little and lose a great deal.
♐	Two people hope that you will be.

The White Magic Book

♃ Look for knotted finger-joints, vanity and untruthfulness.

♄ Generosity which will make you very popular, but which will involve serious sacrifices on your part.

☉ It is sheer folly to fear that.

☿ Yes, but it is pure invention.

♀ Only what you create for yourself.

☽ Yes, but go no further than that.

♋ The longer the delay, the more it will be worth having.

♓ Long before you expect it.

♈ A friend of a member of your family.

♑ It is not exactly enmity. The person is soured by ill-health.

♉ You should have done it long ago.

♎ That you are strong-willed and clear-headed.

♂ Better give the benefit of the doubt.

♌ Yes; but remember that different people see things differently.

♍ Even if you do not give your confidence, you will allow yourself to be robbed of it.

♐ Yes—being more given to thinking than to acting.

The White Magic Book

♃	Yes, and before very long.
♄	Do not worry about past mistakes. It is useless, and very harmful to you.
☉	Your tendency to take offence without cause.
☿	It will demand a great deal of you—and receive it.
♀	You may have to sacrifice a little now, in order to prevent heavy losses later on.
☽	Very—but not for your sake alone.
♋	You are safe. Be content to remain so.
♓	Not when an evasion will serve the purpose better.
♈	You have but to say one word to end it.
♑	The most intellectual man you have ever met.
♉	No; but you will soon cease to regret that.
♎	Graceful—and inclined to vanity.
♂	A woman has suspected—and spoken of it.
♌	Thinks you will probably write a second time.
♍	In the prime of life when he marries.
♐	It does not exist. Personal troubles have caused the change.

The White Magic Book

♃	Better than you have ever hoped for.
♄	The one hundred and seventh day of the year.
☉	You will find a clue very soon now.
☿	It should be one which will keep you in the open air, constantly.
♀	Of a woman whom you will meet some day.
☽	Better do it to-day than to-morrow.
♋	You will not do so much longer.
♓	The keener the anxiety, the sooner it will be over.
♈	Yes, but it will not last long.
♑	It is a matter that need not trouble you.
♉	You will always find your deepest interest in them.
♎	Several small pleasant happenings.
♂	Yes; but try and see from his point of view too.
♌	Yes; but it is impossible to please everyone.
♍	You will have your secret desire.
♐	It depends to a great extent upon a person whom you have not met as yet.

The White Magic Book

♃	Immediately, if you will consider how many are bearing far heavier burdens.
♄	From middle-age onward, in prosperity.
☉	Partly.
☿	It is in a strange place.
♀	One, at least, whom you have never suspected.
☽	No—the second.
♋	You will not have to wait long.
♓	Only unforeseen circumstances delay it.
♈	Your own feeling has failed, or you would not doubt it.
♑	Yes, and more than once.
♉	A discovery which will make you sad, just at first.
♎	They expected that you would do better, financially.
♂	One within the first year.
♌	It will be a great mistake if you do not.
♍	Yes, by means of long nights of sleep in fresh air.
♐	There is no need. You have it.

The White Magic Book

♃	Just as soon as you cease to worry about it.
♄	Do not turn your back on Opportunity because your friends fail to recognise her.
☉	He will wear robes.
☿	Far from it.
♀	No. You never knew that it was once intended for you, so you will never miss it.
☽	Protest, if you must. Then, leave it.
♋	More anxiety, for which you have yourself to blame.
♓	There is, even now, far to go.
♈	More so than you will ever realise.
♑	Yes—now, if you do not delay.
♉	Yes, but you will not like the way it is made.
♎	Not if a third party can prevent it.
♂	Enough to satisfy you—after many disappointments.
♌	Many—by land, by sea, and in the air.
♍	That you are so anxious to get on in the world that it would be hard work to keep up with you.
♐	Yes; and remember that you owe it to yourself to be courteous even when you cannot be kind.

The White Magic Book

♃	Much too soon for your happiness.
♄	You should be on your guard.
☉	Consider your own future also, when you have an impulse to shoulder other people's burdens.
☿	You would be wise to turn your back on the town.
♀	In your own country and near the hills.
☽	It is extremely improbable.
♋	Only partly.
♓	To-day the one, and to-morrow the other.
♈	Let it come without making any apparent effort to help it on.
♑	Yes, in crossing a road.
♉	Good at heart, but very difficult to live with.
♎	Young. Good-looking. Very humorous and popular.
♂	No. Being quite straightforward, it would never occur to him that you were less so.
♌	You must learn to understand him first.
♍	The results will be eventually satisfactory.
♐	Nothing that will surprise you.

The White Magic Book

♃	Yes. More by night than by day.
♄	In the enemy of your friend.
☉	Your dislike of interference.
☿	Be brave and all will go well.
♀	None.
☽	Little griefs which will not last.
♋	Let it be waited for, but grant it in the end.
♓	Anticipation will be the best part of it.
♈	Sooner than will be convenient for some people.
♑	It is the person whom you have in mind.
♉	It is considered that you belong to the opposition.
♎	Go straight about it. Anything else would be fatal.
♂	Clever, and contemptuous of those who are not so.
♌	Yes; and sees no fault in you.
♍	Hope for the best and be prepared for the worst.
♐	You will not find her grateful.

The White Magic Book

♃	The jealousy of another person.
♄	There is no doubt at all about that.
☉	Be bolder and more active in your own behalf.
☿	Extreme sensitiveness. Don't let people see how easily you can be hurt.
♀	With respect—which you will deserve.
☽	Not if you have the courage to abide by your own opinion.
♋	Yes, and will always regret it.
♓	A very short voyage and a safe return.
♈	Occasionally.
♑	Until you decide to act differently.
♉	More persevering than clever.
♎	No. You will have a much stronger wish within twelve months.
♂	Good-looking. Rather dark. Knows something about housekeeping.
♌	There is some suspicion but no blame.
♍	Is wondering whether the letters please you or not.
♐	Between twenty-nine and thirty.

The White Magic Book

♃	Not very soon.
♄	It will be the dearest place on earth to you.
☉	Hundred and forty-second and two hundred and eleventh days of the year.
☿	Wait and everything will be made clear to you.
♀	You would not have done better in any other.
☽	Of a plan to make money.
♋	Yes, but choose a good time.
♓	No. Act decisively before harm comes of it.
♈	There is not much more to endure.
♑	It will not cost you much—nor will it bring you much.
♉	You will soon have one if you do not exercise more self-control.
♎	Yes—more especially when they exist only in your imagination.
♂	News which you do not expect at present.
♌	Very probably; and you will both regret it.
♍	No. You have not done all that you were expected to do.
♐	As you wish, so it will happen to you.

The White Magic Book

♃	Yes, if you are patient.
♄	A speck of dust will clog the mechanism of a watch. Look for your speck of dust—quickly.
☉	Yes, through the exertions of others.
☿	Yes; but remember that to understand all is to forgive all.
♀	It is beyond your reach at present.
☽	Not one, but many.
♋	Unless you do, there will be none.
♓	Yes, to one more envied, but not happier.
♈	Before very long.
♑	If you doubt it, act promptly. Now is the time.
♉	You will be able to escape all such risk if you choose to do so.
♎	A change of quarters.
♂	They sincerely hope that you will be happy.
♌	Two boys.
♍	Never, unless you move from where you are now.
♐	Entirely. Through plain living and interesting work.

The White Magic Book

♃	You have already decided.
♄	Take the trouble to understand a thing thoroughly, and it will never escape you.
☉	Ask for what you want, and never cease asking until you get it.
☿	He will wear a military decoration.
♀	More so than you expect.
☽	It has been bequeathed and revoked; and it will be bequeathed again.
♋	Not unless you have excellent reasons for doing so.
♓	A benefit to you.
♈	Much nearer the end than you think.
♑	You are rather well-known now.
♉	Always—as a result of audacity.
♎	That is what you will marry for; and then you may not benefit.
♂	Some people are greatly against it.
♌	No. Nor will you ever want.
♍	Not until you cross salt water.
♐	That you have a charming speaking-voice.

The White Magic Book

♃	There is nothing to fear because there is nothing to lose.
♄	Yes.
☉	None at present. They will come when your position improves.
☿	Do not expect so much from your friends as you are prepared to do for them.
♀	The country will give you health and fortune.
☽	Here, and near a great river.
♋	You guess what will happen and you will not be disappointed.
♓	To a certain extent.
♈	Both are worthy of respect and affection.
♑	It would benefit neither of you.
♉	Yes. Drink from the left side of your cup when in public places.
♎	Fond of good living and willing to work for it.
♂	Above all, he is one who has learned to make the best of things.
♌	Nothing less than all your attention will satisfy him.
♍	Expect some difficulties at first. Afterwards, you will have all that you desire.
♐	You are clever enough to make it so, if you try.

The White Magic Book

♃	You may do so without running much risk.
♄	No. The mind is solely occupied with worry.
☉	Where there is affection, cowardice and a slovenly tendency.
☿	A credulous nature which will be a constant source of danger.
♀	It has not the slightest foundation.
☽	Not now.
♋	Not more than you have already experienced.
♓	Yes; but insist upon a guarantee for the future.
♈	There has not been leisure to give it a thought.
♑	Too late for some people, too soon for others.
♉	One whom you have often thought about already.
♎	It is thought that things would run more smoothly without you.
♂	Do not hesitate for an instant.
♌	Chiefly, your social qualities are admired.
♍	In the way you mean—yes.
♐	Yes, and time will prove it.

The White Magic Book

♃	Yes; and good-looking.
♄	He has met someone more congenial.
☉	Certainly you will.
☿	You have a leaning toward melancholy. Banish it if you would be happy and prosperous.
♀	Fastidiousness. Remember that it takes all sorts of people to make up a world.
☽	With liberality but not generosity.
♋	Such loss as will not be worth a second thought.
♓	Yes, because your goodwill is much desired.
♈	You are too restless to remain long in one place.
♑	You make it too difficult a task.
♉	No.
♎	Yes. Also cautious and economical.
♂	Think of it continually, live for it, and it will be yours.
♌	Dark-haired, kind-hearted and very self-willed.
♍	Undoubtedly.
♐	Is under the impression that you do not expect to hear yet.

The White Magic Book

♃   Only once, and that will be enough.

♄   You are likely to stay where you are for the present.

☉   You will be very happy in it, and could not desire more.

☿   Seventy-fifth and two hundred and fourteenth days of the year.

♀   Before long, you will know all.

☽   No. You have taken the wrong turning. Try again.

♋   Of a mutual friend.

♓   Wait until enquiries are made. Then, speak out.

♈   It is not to your advantage to do so.

♑   Time alone can deal with them satisfactorily.

♉   What you gain will not be worth having.

♎   You will never have more than rivals of a day.

♂   The mere fact of having them will make you happy.

♌   Hard work and good results from it.

♍   Not always—being aware that he cannot invariably be wrong.

♐   It is the result of envious criticism upon a sensitive nature.

The White Magic Book

♃	Yes. Always sleep on your right side.
♄	It is more than half done. Do not hurry matters on.
☉	Find congenial work—and keep to it.
☿	Peaceful and happy.
♀	They are fairly accurate.
☽	Not far from where you think it is.
♋	Yes—people who are also fond of you.
♓	If you do, you will repent it.
♈	In the course of a year.
♑	Not until you have almost ceased to care whether it arrives or not.
♉	Yes. Remember that still waters run deep.
♎	It is possible. He who breaks, pays.
♂	Success.
♌	They hope much for you, but do not expect a great deal.
♍	Yes, after two years.
♐	Yes, but the man has not reached this country yet.

The White Magic Book

♃	That you are delightful.
♄	Remember that words fly away; but writing remains.
☉	Immediately you realise that a habit of hurrying and a good memory never go together.
☿	Keep your goal in view and never swerve from the path that leads to it.
♀	One in which he will gain honour and fortune.
☽	When the great and inevitable storm is over.
♋	Yes, but not for very many years.
♓	It would be useless to do so.
♈	Not at all what you deserve.
♑	Not soon—but as you wish.
♉	Yes, and much appreciated.
♎	Prosperity is at your door, knocking to come in.
♂	That is what you will believe.
♌	You know that a third person has to be considered.
♍	More than likely—if you decline all advice offered to you.
♐	Yes, and also escapes.

The White Magic Book

♃	The result will not be up to your expectations.
♄	You will only have made one more mistake.
☉	Within twelve months, if you go North.
☿	You have had some, but just now you are free.
♀	Take especial care of your throat and chest.
☽	Both suit you, one as well as the other.
♋	In a land where it seldom rains.
♓	That is not possible without involving someone else.
♈	Quite possible but not certain.
♑	The one who understands you best.
♉	You have already been noticed. Leave it at that.
♎	Never stand near the door of a railway-carriage. Others may escape, but not you.
♂	Inquisitive and wanting in tact, but very affectionate.
♌	Courageous and much liked by his friends. Has been abroad.
♍	Not in the least.
♐	You will never regret having given him the opportunity to try.

The White Magic Book

♃	Some of it, but certainly not all.
♄	She has her own ends in view.
☉	Never has, does not, and never will—in the way you expect.
☿	You need not look far. Hands which close more readily than they open.
♀	A strong objection to advice, however well-meant.
☽	You have nothing to fear.
♋	There will be if you are not careful.
♓	None but what your natural courage will enable you to overcome.
♈	You will do so—not once, but often.
♑	That will depend upon a whim.
♉	Is now preparing to start on a journey.
♎	You will meet within five months.
♂	It is hoped that you will remove yourself to another sphere of activity.
♌	Let your conscience alone guide you in this.
♍	That there is something fascinating about you.
♐	Yes—according to his views.

The White Magic Book

♃	Has already done so.
♄	He carried a sword before you were born.
☉	You are too outspoken. He prefers more kindness and less truth.
☿	Yes, and you will be glad of it.
♀	Do not doubt your own capability or you will poison your whole future.
☽	Reserve. People who might be useful to you are afraid to approach you.
♋	As a welcome guest.
♓	On the contrary, the success of your life is at hand.
♈	The regret is chiefly a matter of courtesy.
♑	Yes, although there will be no necessity.
♉	No, because your comments cut too deeply.
♎	Until you are both very tired of it.
♂	Very; but not energetic enough to profit by it.
♌	There is something far better in store for you.
♍	Extremely sensitive and clever. Has fine eyes.
♐	Make no confidences and there will be absolute safety.

The White Magic Book

♃	Someone has attempted to do so.
♄	Yes.
☉	Circumstances point that way.
☿	You would not exchange it for any other.
♀	One hundred and sixty-third and three hundred and forty-first days of the year.
☽	Do not seek to know or you will regret it.
♋	No. You are in it though force of circumstances.
♓	Very seriously of your future.
♈	Yes; but remember that there are several ways of doing things.
♑	Nothing is worse for you than an unsympathetic environment.
♉	Only through suffering will one of your temperament learn to be strong.
♎	It will bring pleasure unmixed with pain.
♂	A very attractive one.
♌	Yes. Even when they are one-sided.
♍	The discovery that you have made a great mistake.
♐	Yes, if you are unwise enough to shoulder the whole responsibility.

35

The White Magic Book

♃	The later, the better it will be for you.
♄	You have had the best of advice already. Follow it.
☉	Yes—if you acquire good-humour as a habit.
☿	Carry on; and decline to allow anyone to sympathise with you.
♀	You will never regret your youth.
☽	They have some foundation in fact.
♋	It has been hidden.
♓	Events are approaching which will free you from such people.
♈	It will be to your advantage if you do.
♑	Soon; and often.
♉	Immediately after certain important events in your life.
♎	You will find out for certain within the next seven weeks.
♂	Yes, unless you decisively refuse to be drawn into them.
♌	The beginning of a friendship which will bring you much happiness.
♍	They will think that you are making a mistake.
♐	A girl and two boys.

The White Magic Book

♃	Avoid them. They will not bring you happiness, nor health.
♄	It would make you happy if you knew.
☉	Certainly. It must be done.
☿	Cut out hurry and worry from your existence, and there will be no more trouble about that.
♀	First train yourself for it. Your personality will do the rest.
☽	Several before he finds the right one.
♋	When you cease to feel for others, not before.
♓	Yes, when it is no longer a matter of much consequence to you.
♈	It might do more harm than good.
♑	A state of affairs which should make you wiser— but will not.
♉	The end is within sight and right will triumph.
♎	You have done something to deserve general praise—or will do so.
♂	First, you must learn how, when, and where to be generous.
♌	Money, but very little kindness.
♍	You would live to regret it.
♐	You are one of those few who could make riches.

The White Magic Book

♃	He will do his best, but it will be no easy task.
♄	No—chiefly because of a woman.
☉	Do not go.
☿	Not while you remain under the roof which shelters you at present.
♀	Not among men.
☽	You are naturally generous—be wise also.
♋	In the country if you desire happiness.
♓	Over-seas.
♈	No; and you do not really expect that.
♑	It is far from impossible.
♉	Time will show.
♎	Yes.
♂	Be on your guard with all that is keen-edged.
♌	Sympathetic, liberal, impulsive and active.
♍	Downright and outspoken. Rather dark. Quick-tempered.
♐	No. He will be pleased when you are popular.

The White Magic Book

♃	Sometimes, very much so.
♄	You will lose by it if you do not.
☉	She wishes you no ill, but she does think that you may be useful to her.
☿	Not just now. At odd moments, yes.
♀	The person is quick-witted, quick-tempered and given to chattering.
☽	Your liking for domestic life which may lead you to settle down too soon.
♋	Banish it absolutely from your mind or you will make it a reality.
♓	Yes.
♈	Your share—no more.
♑	Yes. No harm was intended.
♉	A gift will come from quite another quarter.
♎	No.
♂	Yes, but it is not the one you hope for.
♌	You are said to be very exacting.
♍	Yes, if you can keep calm and be prepared for anything.
♐	That you could do anything if you put your mind to it.

The White Magic Book

♃	It has been guessed by everybody for a long while.
♄	Other people intervene.
☉	He was born before yourself by ten years.
☿	No need to ask. You know.
♀	Yes. You would have had one before but for an enemy influence.
☽	You have some ambition. Cultivate it if you would succeed.
♋	Accidents to the head.
♓	You will have your due from it, but no more.
♈	No. A great success is almost within your grasp.
♑	There would have been no regret had there been no discovery.
♉	Yes, and you will soon begin them.
♎	You would be surprised if it were so.
♂	Less than a week.
♌	Especially so in argument.
♍	Certainly. You deserve it.
♐	Over twenty-five. Good features. Very outspoken.

The White Magic Book

♃	Insist if you are wise, yield if you would be happy.
♄	No. There is a misunderstanding which can be explained away.
☉	An old man and a young man.
☿	Yes, if another person can manage it.
♀	You will make it to your own liking.
☽	Two hundred and sixty-fourth and three hundred and fiftieth days of the year.
♋	You will do so.
♓	Not unless you are making two blades of grass grow where one grew before.
♈	Of the past, and not with satisfaction.
♑	Be moderate in all things. Even too much candour may be hurtful.
♉	No. It will create unhappiness and continue to do so.
♎	They are already growing less.
♂	To both of you.
☊	Many; but there is safety in numbers.
♍	With your temperament, you could not be otherwise.
♐	Exactly what you have been expecting for some time.

41

The White Magic Book

♃	Three.
♄	Yes.
☉	It depends entirely upon yourself. Be very hopeful.
☿	It is possible at present, but it will not be later on.
♀	Find your patch of sunshine and fix your thoughts firmly on that.
☽	As much so as your youth.
♋	Yes; but you are advised never to mention them.
♓	It is in the open.
♈	Several people—whom you know but slightly.
♑	Do what you consider is right, not what you think may be expedient.
♉	During the waning of a moon.
♎	The affair drags, and definite information is impossible.
♂	More if possible.
♌	You will have no alternative if you wish to protect your rights.
♍	Many new experiences and not all pleasant ones.
♐	Only a very few take any real interest in the matter.

The White Magic Book

♃ Great fortune and yourself will never come together.

♄ Yes, but they will not end fortunately for you.

☉ That you are above criticism.

☿ Yes, in as few words as possible.

♀ Yes. Never allow your thoughts to wander from what is your actual occupation at the moment.

☽ Create a demand—then supply it.

♋ Rather a dangerous one, and you will be proud of it.

♓ Much more so than you desire.

♈ Someone certainly does consider the advisability of benefiting you in that way.

♑ If you are quite sure that you have more experience and more brain-power—not otherwise.

♉ Less disastrous than you suppose.

♎ When a certain person's doubts have been satisfied.

♂ Yes, as one who is always ready to do a kindness.

♌ Yes. Personal popularity goes a long way.

♍ Money matters will continuously improve.

♐ At present, no one wishes it but yourself.

The White Magic Book

♃	Not without good cause.
♄	Not so much so as you deserve.
☉	There will be some trifling vexations.
☿	First pleasure and then acute annoyance.
♀	Very soon indeed.
☽	There are envious women about you.
♋	Don't try to shut your eyes again when once they have been opened. That is moral cowardice.
♓	Far from town you will find good health, prosperity and happiness.
♈	In an English town, near the sea.
♑	You will be told just what it is considered expedient that you should know.
♉	Within the year, if at all.
♎	Both sincerely admire you.
♂	Yes; and then you will be only one of the many.
♌	Your special danger will be where a lighted match has been thrown down.
♍	Inclined to melancholy and disposed to a quiet life.
♐	Smokes incessantly and is a great reader.

The White Magic Book

♃	That you are very easily influenced.
♄	Your kindnesses are borne in mind.
☉	There is no need to doubt.
☿	Her motive will not bear examination.
♀	Too much for peace of mind.
☽	Has short thick fingers, short nails, and could be very cruel.
♋	Your slowness in making a decision.
♓	Do what is right and fear nothing.
♈	No; but about someone with whom you are closely connected.
♑	No. You are one of the fortunate ones, though you may not think so.
♉	It will have no good results, if you do.
♎	There is a strong wish to offer you one, but doubt as to whether you will accept it.
♂	When it is permitted.
♌	No.
♍	You have too many friends to please that person.
♐	If you feel that you are justified, go right on.

The White Magic Book

♃	Slender and not very tall.
♄	People believe what you wished them to believe.
☉	There is no reason at all.
☿	As young as yourself.
♀	A previous claim.
☽	Yes. You ought to have had one before this.
♋	You can make excellent plans. Be strong enough to carry them out.
♓	Lack of perseverance when things persistently go wrong.
♈	You will get your rights, but no favours.
♑	No. Success will be heaped upon success.
♉	Would appear to be so when in your presence.
♎	One only, which will be very eventful.
♂	You have already made up your mind on that point.
♌	It may. Do not leave it until it is too late.
♍	Only in the art of making money.
♐	Yes, when you have almost ceased to hope for it.

The White Magic Book

♃	Some annoyances—none of which need disturb you.
♄	There is always time to yield, but it is sometimes too late to be firm.
☉	Yes, but not intentionally.
☿	Once—and that you will consider once too often.
♀	It will be all to your advantage to go.
☽	You will be thankful for it every day of your life.
♋	Two hundred and thirty-fourth; and two hundred and forty-first.
♓	Some of it—not all.
♈	You need scope for your undoubted talent for business.
♑	Building castles in the air—and peopling them.
♉	Nothing will be gained by hiding the truth.
♎	No. Force your way out of the difficulty.
♂	Until you have thoroughly learned a lesson which will be very valuable to you in the future.
☊	You will always be glad that it happened.
♍	You have had them and will have them.
♐	If you know exactly where to stop.

The White Magic Book

♃	Some of them will be.
♄	Yes, that is certain.
☉	Happily for you, yes.
☿	Yes. Sleep with your head toward the magnetic North.
♀	You can do so.
☽	Yes, if you will remember that sunlight breaks through the darkest clouds.
♋	You will have an assured position.
♓	Not entirely.
♈	It is awaiting enquiry.
♑	Yes; because the person in question is very conscious of inferiority.
♉	You should do so, but probably will not.
♎	Yes, for the better.
♂	At any moment.
♌	You do not doubt it at all.
♍	As the past has been, so will the future be in this respect.
♐	A gradual improvement of all your circumstances.

The White Magic Book

♃	Yes; and someone else also.
♄	No; but will have an adequate income.
☉	You will look for many but find few.
☿	That you mean more than you say.
♀	It is necessary, but be very careful.
☽	Don't accept heavy undertakings, and improvement will begin at once.
♋	Take your wares to the best market, however far it may be.
♓	One which will keep him away from you a great deal.
♈	Where you are, peace is not.
♑	Yes, but you will not like the way in which it will come.
♉	Remember that the responsibility lies with him.
♎	An imprint on the rest of your life.
♂	When it is realised that the end which was at first desired must be abandoned.
♌	Yes, to hundreds, but not to thousands.
♍	Your choice of a business is the main point. Therein lies success—or disaster.
♐	When the time comes, it will never trouble you.

The White Magic Book

♃	Is good-tempered though not good-looking. Has worked under Government.
♄	Just at first. Not later on.
☉	Yes.
☿	On the whole, you will be glad that you went.
♀	Nothing will be gained—by you.
☽	A woman prevents it.
♋	Only one who need cause any anxiety.
♓	You are very straightforward—do not expect everyone to be the same.
♈	You will take happiness with you wherever you go.
♑	Here, in the Midlands.
♉	No; but you might get it elsewhere.
♎	No. The cause will be someone whom you will never meet.
♂	The one who sometimes disagrees with you.
♌	There is no insurmountable obstacle.
♍	You will have to be very cautious in the first three months of the year.
♐	Has energy, ardour, and a very strong will.

The White Magic Book

♃	As soon as possible.
♄	That you are clever, but not kind.
☉	Entirely.
☿	There is truth in it.
♀	She may be a pleasant companion. Stop there.
☽	Yes, being unable to avoid doing so.
♋	Has rather large hands and a small handwriting.
♓	Your readiness to make friends.
♈	Destroy the fear, and you will conquer all along the line.
♑	Be more discreet. If you touch pitch, you must be defiled.
♉	You can avoid it—by exercising your judgment when the time comes.
♎	Now or never.
♂	It is thought that such a gift must necessarily be followed by others.
♌	There is no certainty at present. Be prepared.
♍	You will not meet for two years yet.
♐	That will be shown to you very clearly before long.

The White Magic Book

♃	After many years.
♄	Thick eyelashes and a charming smile.
☉	A secret known to two is no longer a secret.
☿	Sheer disinclination to do so.
♀	No.
☽	The fear lest you should come to mean too much to him.
♋	But for an error of judgment on your part, you would have been in it by now.
♓	A little selfishness is a good thing, whatever altruists may say; but stop at a little.
♈	Your fancy for being a law unto yourself.
♑	Hospitably.
♉	No. A lack of courage now will be followed by lasting regret.
♎	Profoundly so.
♂	Several between here and the West.
♌	You have excellent reason to know.
♍	The longer the worse for you.
♐	Yes, chiefly in very modern subjects.

The White Magic Book

♃	Love and happiness are not always the same thing.
♄	A surprise, but not an unpleasant one.
☉	With a little management, you may satisfy both.
☿	You have already guessed the truth.
♀	One whom you will govern, and one who will govern you.
☽	It is more than likely.
♋	You will find peace there, and comfort also.
♓	The seventeenth and fiftieth days of the year.
♈	Others know, and so will you in time.
♑	You would do well to keep to it.
♉	An old quarrel.
♎	Let the matter rest.
♂	You realised that it was a mistake, long ago.
☊	Until an enemy influence is removed.
♍	What is good for one will be good for both.
♐	Yes; but they pass.

The White Magic Book

♃	The greatest happiness of your life, so far.
♄	Generally—yes.
☉	Three, and two of them good-looking.
☿	Not in extreme youth.
♀	There is no doubt about it. Bear that in mind.
☽	Quite easily.
♋	When you learn to control your emotions instead of allowing them to master you.
♓	If you make a hard bed for yourself, you must lie on it—so be wise in time.
♈	There is an atom of truth in them—and the rest is prejudice.
♑	It is not now where you lost it.
♉	Yes; but only the envious one will suffer.
♎	Yes, and lose no time in doing so.
♂	It should have been changed before now. Search for the cause.
♌	Too soon for your comfort.
♍	Think it over. No one knows better than yourself.
♐	Yes, but the prospect need not trouble you.

The White Magic Book

♃	There will be neither riches nor poverty.
♄	Both must agree to that.
☉	Not so much so as you merit.
☿	Enough to teach you the danger of them.
♀	That you are more sensible than affectionate.
☽	It will make no difference, one way or the other.
♋	It will return when your general health becomes normal.
♓	By always having two strings to your bow.
♈	He will have two, one of which will give excellent results.
♑	No. You would find it wearisome.
♉	Yes, but not a large one.
♎	If you are thoroughly convinced of their folly—not otherwise.
♂	Freedom from similar anxiety in the future.
♌	When certain people have been convinced that they cannot do exactly as they wish.
♍	Not in youth, but later on.
♐	Yes, if you can recognise Fortune when it stares you in the face.

The White Magic Book

♃	Clever, idle, and good-tempered.
♄	Has small independent means.
☉	Always—of everybody.
☿	He will consider his own happiness before yours.
♀	Most of the pleasure will fall to your share.
☽	Nothing that will frighten you.
♋	Yes, but not for the last time.
♓	The worst one is yourself.
♈	To bear in mind that it is unlikely that you are always in the right.
♑	There is fortune for you in the country. Go and get it.
♉	You will go to the East before you settle down in prosperity.
♎	Emphatically, you are advised to leave it alone.
♂	It will.
♌	The outspoken one.
♍	If you go the right way—not an easy thing to do.
♐	Avoid the darkness.

The White Magic Book

♃	You are in the way.
♄	Consider it a great deal more yet.
☉	Opinions on this point are as far asunder as the Poles.
☿	Has always been and always will be.
♀	It will be unfortunate for you if you do not.
☽	Make no confidences and you will have nothing to regret.
♋	Much more often than you think of that person.
♓	In one who admires order and tidiness, but does not practise either.
♈	Sincerity—which blinds you to insincerity of others.
♑	Less than ever.
♉	Only by people who defame everybody.
♎	When you allow others to make you joyful, you give them also the power to bring you sadness.
♂	If you can do so freely.
♌	Deep consideration is being given to the matter.
♍	It is more likely now than it has been for a long while.
♐	Yes; and you know that you have done so.

The White Magic Book

♃   Enough brains to be able to look after himself and after you also.

♄   Yes—when it is no longer your heart's desire.

☉   Serious eyes, and a low-pitched voice.

☿   It will not be discovered during your life-time.

♀   Through indisposition—which will pass.

☽   It is said that young ones are not always the best. You will be able to judge for yourself.

♋   Has an idea that you are inclined to be extravagant.

♓   You will share it with one other person.

♈   Bear in mind that you will have wasted your energy if you stop working before success comes.

♑   Contempt for other people's point of view.

♉   As one who is very well-liked.

♎   Not unless you refuse business which will shortly be put before you.

♂   Would do practically anything to put matters right.

☊   One very long one, with no return for many years.

♍   Look nearer for an informant.

♐   It may last for ever if you are obstinate.

The White Magic Book

♃	You have had them, but that is all over now.
♄	Both happy and unhappy.
☉	A short journey with a pleasant ending to it.
☿	One conscience cannot guide two people.
♀	No. It is a cloud which will pass.
☽	As often as you wish; but you would be better alone.
♋	Yes, if you are wise.
♓	It will realise your strongest wish.
♈	The two hundred and seventy-fifth day of the year.
♑	It will remain a secret—for excellent reasons.
♉	Go on with it.
♎	An injury which should have been forgotten long ago.
♂	It would be easing yourself to disturb someone else.
♌	You have an alternative. Take it.
♍	They must run their full course.
♐	Yes, if you do not concede quite all that is asked.

The White Magic Book

♃	Yes, as a witness—and an unwilling one.
♄	Increase of fortune.
☉	They will say one thing and think another.
☿	One.
♀	You will look very much younger than your years.
☽	You know exactly what to do to ensure it. Do it.
♋	You have only to make your preference clear.
♓	When you make your imagination your servant. At present, it rules you.
♈	It will be very different from your youth.
♑	Dismiss them from your mind. This is sound advice.
♉	It is under the stars.
♎	Yes; but you have got your horse by the bridle, and need fear no one.
♂	Yes, you will never regret it.
♌	A man will help you—and before long.
♍	It may not come for a long while yet.
♐	Yes; and it is within your power to become more so.

The White Magic Book

♃	You will sail against wind and tide, but you will make harbour at last.
♄	No; but where love is.
☉	There is an insurmountable obstacle to that marriage.
☿	Yes, if you trust to your own judgment.
♀	You will have more than one which you will prefer not to mention.
☽	Very kind and good-humoured, but might be wiser.
♋	It would be a mistake to do so.
♓	Yes, if you can manage to be more alone.
♈	Specialise in what you *can* do—not in what your friends think that you can do.
♑	He will have no need to work, but he will do so.
♉	You do not wish it. Your mind is too active.
♎	You will have a share in one.
♂	Consult each other before any decisions are made.
♌	That which you hope for.
♍	Very suddenly, but not unsatisfactorily.
♐	No, because at heart you dislike the glare of publicity.

The White Magic Book

♃	Not if you are always on your guard with women.
♄	Careless, affectionate, and liberal.
☉	Very quick-witted. Has dark hair and a good figure.
☿	No—having perfect trust in you.
♀	Yes, if love is all you need.
☽	Yes, if you are very careful the whole of the time.
♋	No harm if you are very discreet.
♓	You have missed one chance and will probably miss another.
♈	No. Probably, you never will have any.
♑	Be guided more by your brain, and less by your emotions.
♉	There is danger for you in the town, especially in the town by the sea.
♎	In one of the greatest cities of the world.
♂	No, because it is not considered to be due to you.
♌	There is no reason against it, at present.
♍	The one who is so easily offended.
♐	You could do so; but it would not lead to what you wish.

The White Magic Book

♃	Yes, in one whom you know very well.
♄	Not seeing any superiority, you do not appear to admit it.
☉	If you are quite sure that you have patience and strength to see it through— yes.
☿	That you are attractive and intend to be so.
♀	Has been more so than will ever be the case again.
☽	It would be wise to do so.
♋	She means well, but she has her limitations.
♓	Thinks of you, and dreams of you, sometimes.
♈	Has an irritable temper, obstinate will, and short thumbs.
♑	An inclination to melancholy—which should be kept in check.
♉	It never had any foundation.
♎	You will not escape altogether.
♂	The griefs that all humanity have in common.
♌	Yes; but you can never trust as before.
♍	There is a fear lest you should think it necessary to make some adequate return.
♐	The time of departure is definitely fixed.

The White Magic Book

♃	Long enough for the end of it to be a great relief.
♄	Quite as much so as yourself.
☉	Yes, in full measure.
☿	Has a pretty wit.
♀	Yes, while you retain control of your willpower.
☽	Something you wrote did not please. Leave it there and nothing will come of it.
♋	Yes, and that will be his chief merit.
♓	Untruthful rumours.
♈	You could have it now, easily, if you understood how to go about it.
♑	Make no confidences. Most people do not think as you do, no matter what they pretend.
♉	A love of beauty which may lead you into difficulties.
♎	It will freely recognise all your good points.
♂	Very unlikely indeed.
♌	Yes, for reasons which you will never understand.
♍	Not many, but a few.
♐	Observe that person's custom with others.

The White Magic Book

♃	It will be pleasant, but not advantageous to you.
♄	Not at the present time.
☉	Love has never been the road to unalloyed happiness.
☿	A letter which you will be glad to receive.
♀	Go half-way, and you will be met.
☽	A sense of injury certainly does exist.
♋	No.
♓	It needs courage, but it would benefit you in every way.
♈	It will express yourself in every way, and therefore you will love it.
♑	The two-hundred and sixtieth day of the year.
♉	Not the whole truth.
♎	To excel in the one for which you were better fitted, you should have been trained from childhood.
♂	Someone very recently met, and much liked.
♌	Yes. Justice demands it.
♍	It is not good for you; but consider very carefully before you act.
♐	No. The worst is over.

The White Magic Book

♃   Quite; but when the prize has been won there is no more racing for it.

♄   To a small extent and you will be unable to avoid it.

☉   A new friend who will give a new turn to your thoughts.

☿   Some will wonder at your choice.

♀   No.

☽   Quite young, but not young enough to please you.

♋   Yes, when you learn to break your fast with cold water.

♓   There are obstacles; but they can be overcome.

♈   Yes, and very soon.

♑   Trust to yourself to make it so, and it will be.

♉   Yes.

♎   There is a roof above it.

♂   One who cannot help being so, but who wishes you no harm.

♌   If you can do so without losing your self-respect.

♍   Yes, and your environment will be much more pleasant.

♐   Toward night.

The White Magic Book

♃	You or your work will always be before the public more or less.
♄	Yes, in spite of many errors of judgment.
☉	Yes, you will be rich—in money.
☿	You will not if you are wise.
♀	Fortune will come to you while you are sleeping.
☽	Yes, but the pleasure of the first one is unlikely to be repeated.
♋	So much, that disillusion may follow.
♓	Yes, or you will regret it later on.
♈	The power is still there. Rush and scurry have only veiled it.
♑	By not abusing power when it is entrusted to you.
♉	You will call it a profession, others may call it a trade.
♎	Not unless you are content to live alone.
♂	Some of your fortune lies in the roadway. Be careful not to pass over it.
♌	If you do not approve, do not be persuaded.
♍	On the whole, a favourable conclusion for you.
♐	Directly one person who is involved realises what failure means.

The White Magic Book

♃	It is highly improbable.
♄	Look for it where there are wheels.
☉	Subtle, well-mannered and self-reliant.
☿	Medium colouring and exceptionally pleasant manner. Wears ring on fourth finger.
♀	No. He will never have any reason to be.
☽	You will never know sorrow when you are with him.
♋	Not from your point of view.
♓	Nothing at all if you are strong. Disaster if you are weak.
♈	Yes, and very happily.
♑	Yes, but they will never be able to harm you.
♉	You have a strong sense of duty— but you should consider your own interests also.
♎	The country, over-sea.
♂	Where you will—prosperity goes with you.
♌	Yes, if you demand it.
♍	Yes; but the mainspring must be set in motion first.
♐	The one whose enemies are also your enemies.

The White Magic Book

♃	There is no thought of return at present.
♄	Your affinity is in another country now.
☉	Envy—no more, no less.
☿	Leave it as long as possible.
♀	That you are likely to be well worth knowing some day.
☽	Yes.
♋	You know that it is true.
♓	Remember what happened on a previous occasion.
♈	Yes, and is very unhappy over it.
♑	Is ambitious, unattractive, and fond of domineering over people.
♉	Deep and strong emotions which must not be allowed to master your reasoning power.
♎	That fear is simply the product of an unhealthy imagination.
♂	There will be if you are not more reserved in your conversation with women.
♌	Sorrow, but not misfortune.
♍	Do not harbour ill-will; but profit by your experience.
♐	It has been suggested that to send it would put you in a position which you would resent.

The White Magic Book

♃	Is as truthful as yourself.
♄	Until you make an advance.
☉	Sufficiently so to make his fortune.
☿	When it becomes possible, it will have been replaced by another.
♀	Brown-haired, over twenty, and clever at nursing.
☽	It is already known.
♋	You are out of sight and therefore out of mind.
♓	Not much more than a boy, but still your master.
♈	Your somewhat harsh criticism of other people.
♑	Yes. A man and a woman will bring it about.
♉	You are keen enough to see other people's bad points. Be clever enough not to talk about them.
♎	Your quick temper—which, however, is not an unforgiving one.
♂	As one whom it would be much better not to offend.
♌	Not if you remember that to lend money ends friendship.
♍	Yes. The memory of it will always hurt, more or less.
♐	Not yet, and not very many.

The White Magic Book

♃	They are but clouds which will soon vanish.
♄	It will cost you more sorrow than happiness, eventually.
☉	One only, who is not dangerous.
☿	Not altogether—and through your own fault.
♀	A little gift made with much kindness.
☽	No. There should be give and take in all things.
♋	You forget that silence is golden.
♓	As often as your first husband will have married when he marries you.
♈	It was settled some time ago, without reference to you.
♑	You will see no fault in it.
♉	The two hundredth day of the year.
♎	Yes.
♂	Go out into the world and something much better will present itself.
♌	Of you.
♍	Consider how it will affect everyone before you speak.
♐	If you are strong enough to endure, it will be better for you in the end.

The White Magic Book

♃	Better for you to be without it.
♄	If not, it is your own fault.
☉	Yes, but there will be no publicity.
☿	A great improvement in health.
♀	No. You cannot expect to please everyone.
☽	Several.
♋	You will have to wait some time yet.
♓	Seek sunshine continually—think of sunshine and you will have your wish.
♈	Yes.
♑	Yes. Love will help you to do that.
♉	You will have adequate means.
♎	Consider the matter again before you call them *suspicious*.
♂	It is being conveyed, still unseen, from place to place.
♌	There are some who fear that you will give them cause for envy yet.
♍	Make very sure first that one is desired.
♐	An opportunity will soon present itself. Take it.

The White Magic Book

♃	Much sooner than anyone could have expected.
♄	Only in a small circle.
☉	There are reverses for you. Also success.
☿	No, but prosperity will come later in life.
♀	No, nor anyone else at present.
☽	Yes; but you will have to wait for it.
♋	Yes, but always remember that there is a road which may end in a precipice.
♓	He thinks he has found absolute perfection, but he will modify that opinion before long.
♈	Wait seven days before doing so.
♑	Yes—if for a time you live by a simple routine, and do not vary it.
♉	Go your own way and pay no attention to criticism.
♎	He will wear a sword or has worn one.
♂	It might be, but others will bring the storms into it.
☊	It will come to you through a trifling speculation.
♍	Judge the prospects of the future by the experience you have had in the past.
♐	A better one than you have any reason to look for.

The White Magic Book

♃	The one whom you knew first.
♄	Do not try. Your feeling would not be reciprocated.
☉	Yes, in the ordinary risks of the road.
☿	Hot-tempered, outspoken, and fond of domestic comfort.
♀	Pale and has a stern expression. Somewhat abrupt in manner.
☽	More jealous than loving.
♋	Yes, if you can content yourself with little.
♓	Someone will be pleased even if you are not.
♈	Pleasure only—if you know how to keep a tight hand on the reins.
♑	Someone is thinking about it, and only needs a little encouragement.
♉	Yes, but they fear you too much to become active.
♎	Exercise much more caution in making new friends.
♂	Town in the Western world.
♌	Near any city.
♍	No. Something will be kept back.
♐	Circumstances are steadily against it—and *yet* it may be.

The White Magic Book

♃	You will have to wait some time yet.
♄	No. Nor is there any wish to do so.
☉	You will go from one whom you know, to one as yet unknown.
☿	Words which you never intended to be repeated.
♀	No. Give it up.
☽	That you are extremely interesting.
♋	Wishes to be, but cannot.
♓	Without reserve.
♈	Chiefly, she wishes to make the acquaintance of your friends.
♑	Yes, and is becoming more and more puzzled.
♉	Has a morbid imagination and takes pleasure in horrors.
♎	Your excellent powers of judgment.
♂	No. Whenever it enters your mind, crush it, and think of something beautiful.
♌	Yes, without fail, sooner or later.
♍	The sorrows of others will be your chief burden.
♐	Yes; but in future be on your guard.

The White Magic Book

♃	Long and short and fairly often.
♄	Only by accident.
☉	It would last for ever if you were wise.
☿	You will be quite certain of it.
♀	It is highly improbable at present.
☽	Dark hair, dark eyes and very red lips. Quick temper.
♋	If it is not known now, it never will be.
♓	There are excellent reasons which you will learn later.
♈	He was born in the same year as yourself.
♑	A careless remark which was never intended to wound.
♉	Someone who is very fond of you will make that certain.
♎	Be satisfied with love and do not crave for worship.
♂	It is your nature to seek the very best; but do not turn from anything less with disgust.
♌	It will approve of you.
♍	No. Fortune approaches you with gold in both hands.
♐	Not at all.

The White Magic Book

♃	You would be happier elsewhere.
♄	Be strong and you will have nothing to fear.
☉	It will be the cause of great happiness.
☿	You are surrounded by them, yet will remain unharmed.
♀	No doubt of it. They are the chief interest of your life.
☽	Unavoidable disappointment which will spur you on to try again.
♋	When it happens to be the same as his own.
♓	What you did say is not exactly the same as has been reported.
♈	Three times if you marry this year.
♑	Several people wish it, and may possibly bring it about.
♉	It will entirely content you.
♎	The two hundred and seventh day of the year.
♂	No. Every precaution has been taken to prevent that.
♌	You know what you want. Keep on trying for it.
♍	That "all is vanity."
♐	In such a case, silence would be best.

The White Magic Book

♃	It is now as it should be for your ultimate benefit.
♄	While you must wait, days may run into months.
☉	Sometimes more, sometimes less.
☿	Yes. A very trifling matter, but vexatious.
♀	Fresh interests and new plans which will have good results.
☽	There are only two people whom you need consider.
♋	Every year for many years.
♓	You will have more than one opportunity to do so.
♈	Yes—when you let it come to you through open windows.
♑	You may; but you are not the only one who desires it.
♉	Yes. Fix your thoughts on something that would make you happy and wish for that.
♎	You will have everything to make it so.
♂	Time will show. Meanwhile, keep silence.
♌	It has not yet been discovered.
♍	Yes. One who envies many people.
♐	No; but let it be seen that you harbour no ill feelings.

The White Magic Book

♃	Exactly what you have expected from the first.
♄	It is impossible that it should last much longer.
☉	Yes.
☿	You will lose at first, but afterward there will be great gain.
♀	You will miss all that makes life worth having if you wait for that.
☽	If you are not already engaged, you soon will be.
♋	Do not expect it.
♓	You will have many.
♈	That you are the only one who could make him happy.
♑	No.
♉	Yes, when you have a place for everything and keep everything in its place.
♎	Be resolute, self-reliant and self-contained.
♂	He will wear a silk gown.
♌	Enough so to rest you after the storm.
♍	Yes—as a reward for a kind action.
♐	If you see any possibility of a good ending, however slight, do not be discouraging.

The White Magic Book

♃	No—very fortunately for you.
♄	The elder.
☉	You may do so; but it would not benefit you in any way.
☿	Do not travel by sea for two years yet.
♀	One to harbour a grudge even when he does not seem to take offence.
☽	Has steady eyes and does not talk much. Over thirty.
♋	Yes. He will believe more in your love than in your wisdom.
♓	Everywhere and at all times and places.
♈	Moderately—no more.
♑	The gathering of Dead Sea fruit which will turn to ashes.
♉	Yes; but much as you now wish it, you will soon regret it.
♎	Yes. If you were less straightforward, they would like you better.
♂	Repress your tendency to brood over troubles—especially past ones.
♌	A town very far away.
♍	Health and happiness here. Fortune across the sea.
♐	You have never had that and you never will.

The White Magic Book

♃	Forgive—as you would wish to be forgiven under similar circumstances.
♄	Possibly never.
☉	On the contrary is going further away first.
☿	He knows you better than you know him.
♀	Merely difference of disposition. You are better apart.
☽	It is the best idea that you have ever had.
♋	That you need more self-control.
♓	Is faithful only to pleasure wherever it is to be found.
♈	Entirely.
♑	Be cautious. She is deeper than she appears to be.
♉	Not now; but you could bring it about if you cared to do so.
♎	In one who is chiefly interested in making a good appearance.
♂	A gift for reading character almost at a glance.
♌	No. Put it away, it is unworthy of you.
♍	Yes; and by those who might be expected to know better.
♐	Nothing that could be dignified by the name of sorrow.

The White Magic Book

♃	No. It is a mere pretence.
♄	Yes, if you are not wise enough to dispense with them.
☉	When it is likely to please you.
☿	A few days and nights.
♀	Of average mentality.
☽	Yes.
♋	Has a keen sense of humour. Good figure Nearing thirty.
♓	When it ceases to be one there will be no unpleasant consequences for you.
♈	You will never know the exact truth about that.
♑	In the thirties.
♉	It is a matter of expediency.
♎	Yes. Influences from the North and South will bring that about.
♂	Always bear in mind that it is possible to set too high a value upon money.
♌	The belief that some people are all good and others are quite worthless.
♍	As one who will not be moved from a considered purpose.
♐	Keep love affairs and money matters widely apart and you will be safe.

The White Magic Book

♃	Think over all the probable consequences first.
♄	It is harmful to you.
☉	As long as they are serious.
☿	It will bring you health and prosperity.
♀	Several, but you will have an easy victory.
☽	That will depend upon how you manage them.
♋	Not what you expect.
♓	You will generally see eye to eye.
♈	You should be much more careful what you say.
♑	You will have the opportunity to do so.
♉	You are better where you are. Be very sure of that.
♎	Anyone might envy you the happiness which it will give you.
♂	The two hundred and first day of the year.
♌	Not until your feeling on that subject has changed considerably.
♍	You might have made more money in another line of life, but you are far better as it is.
♐	About to-morrow.

The White Magic Book

♃	There is no other way of arriving at it.
♄	It will change slowly for the better.
☉	Its passage is delayed, but it is well on the way.
☿	It was admiration at first. Now, it is love.
♀	It will go no further than threats.
☽	Nothing that need disturb you in any way.
♋	More surprised than pleased.
♓	Yes; and the youngest will become famous.
♈	Not very. You are too difficult to please.
♑	Be courageous and calm. Anger or despair create actual poison in the blood.
♉	It is not to be won; but it will be given.
♎	Yes. Try to make someone else less sad.
♂	You will have done your duty and you will have your reward.
♌	Wait a little while and you will be quite sure.
♍	There are locks and keys between you and it.
♐	Yes—chiefly of your power of making friends.

The White Magic Book

♃	Not unless you wish for disaster.
♄	Nothing undesirable. On the contrary.
☉	Do not expect an ending at present.
☿	Yes, quite suddenly.
♀	If you persevere, the result will be as you wish.
☽	You will be able to choose. With riches there will be jealousy and meanness.
♋	It is your best chance of happiness.
♓	Money will come to you, but you will never keep it.
♈	The first few will give you a distaste for more.
♑	That you are merely amusing yourself with him.
♉	There will be another. Wait for that.
♎	Control yourself firmly and the power will return gradually and certainly.
♂	Be careful not to make any more enemies.
♌	His chief income will come from the land.
♍	What some call peace, you would consider stagnation.
♐	Yes, but more probably as a gift than as a right.

The White Magic Book

♃	It would be useless to expect it.
♄	No. The result would be less gratifying than you can imagine.
☉	The one who appeared less interested in you at first.
☿	Do not dwell upon the idea. It would only cause you harm.
♀	Go slowly wherever you may be. Swiftness is the danger.
☽	Has a tendency to grumble—which you will cure.
♋	Tall and slightly grey. Very courteous in manner.
♓	In so far as he will fear your love of admiration.
♈	Money will be the difficulty, but you can get over that if you try.
♑	A success for you—if you will remember that a still tongue makes a wise head.
♉	That you will be cured of an infatuation.
♎	Yes; but it will not last long.
♂	Yes— of all ages.
♌	Do not be drawn into worries which do not especially concern you.
♍	Country, in a land which you have never yet seen.
♐	In Central Europe.

The White Magic Book

♃	Yes; but to suffer and to experience joy is to live.
♄	It would be a mistake to be too severe.
☉	Too soon, for you will be disappointed.
☿	As soon as it is in any way possible.
♀	You have known each other for some little time.
☽	You appear to lead opinion against that person.
♋	Do not be hasty. Waiting will do no harm.
♓	That in need, you would be a good friend.
♈	That quality was first lost for your sake.
♑	You do not doubt it.
♉	There is always time to bestow trust. Be cautious.
♎	Only when you meet.
♂	In one who is under the impression that all who behold, admire.
♌	The power to endure.
♍	You would not speak of it—therefore, do not think of it.
♐	Yes—especially when good fortune comes your way.

The White Magic Book

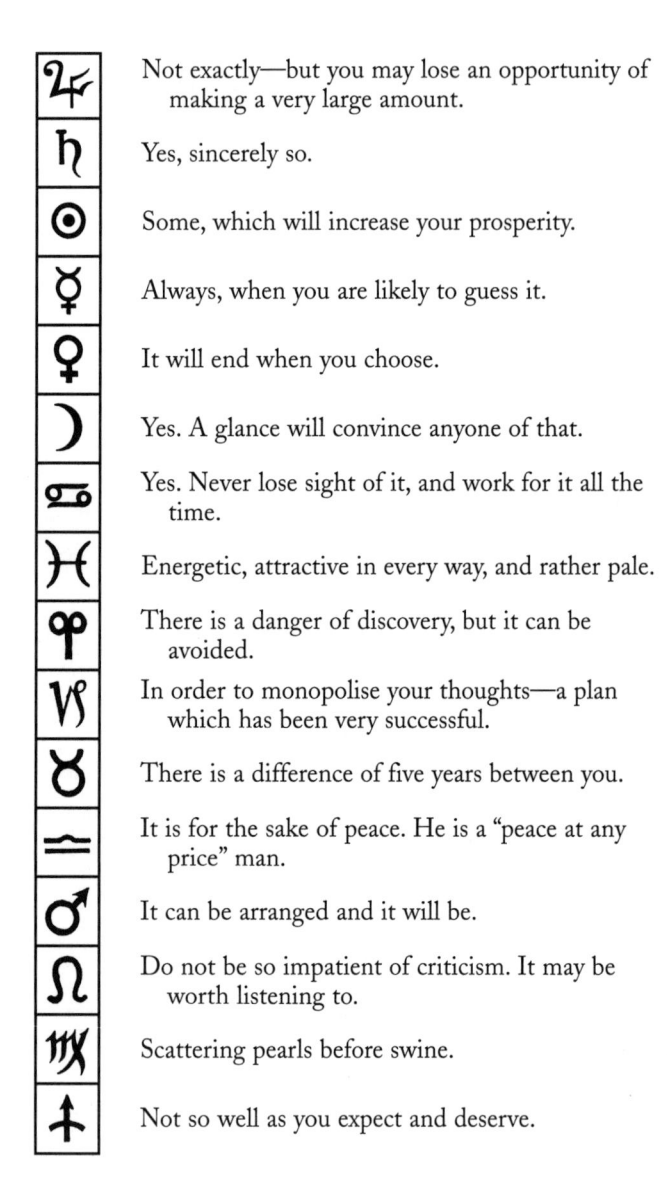

♃	Not exactly—but you may lose an opportunity of making a very large amount.
♄	Yes, sincerely so.
☉	Some, which will increase your prosperity.
☿	Always, when you are likely to guess it.
♀	It will end when you choose.
☽	Yes. A glance will convince anyone of that.
♋	Yes. Never lose sight of it, and work for it all the time.
♓	Energetic, attractive in every way, and rather pale.
♈	There is a danger of discovery, but it can be avoided.
♑	In order to monopolise your thoughts—a plan which has been very successful.
♉	There is a difference of five years between you.
♎	It is for the sake of peace. He is a "peace at any price" man.
♂	It can be arranged and it will be.
♌	Do not be so impatient of criticism. It may be worth listening to.
♍	Scattering pearls before swine.
♐	Not so well as you expect and deserve.

The White Magic Book

♃	Not of you, but very kindly of someone else.
♄	If you tell that which you have in mind, you will have to tell a great deal more.
☉	Try again. It will be good for you to do so.
☿	Not so long as they have already lasted.
♀	You will gain nothing by it.
☽	Two, one of whom is your equal.
♋	Yes. Nothing will prevent that.
♓	A change of occupation.
♈	If he yields to-day, he will insist to-morrow.
♑	Evil tongues and evil minds.
♉	You will not, even if you can.
♎	When you have ceased to think about it.
♂	Yes. Once in it, you will shut the door against troubles.
♌	The hundred and thirty-second day of the year.
♍	No.
♐	No, it was a mistake from the beginning.

The White Magic Book

♃ Yes, of your influence in certain quarters.

♄ Certainly—as you happen to be in the wrong.

☉ It will change for the worse if you are not careful.

☿ During an afternoon.

♀ There is friendship in addition now.

☽ Yes, but the case will be withdrawn from the list.

♋ Something which you have always wished for.

♓ They will be sincerely glad.

♈ Six.

♑ Not under twenty.

♉ Everything is in your favour. *Persevere.*

♎ Yes, certainly; but someone intervenes.

♂ By leaving yourself no leisure for sadness.

♌ As much so as you deserve.

♍ You have no reason for doubting it.

♐ The surmise you have formed on the subject is correct.

The White Magic Book

♃ Quite possibly; but those who wait for dead men's shoes often go barefoot a long while.

♄ Do not interfere unless you are prepared to take all the consequences.

☉ Only what will pass and be forgotten.

☿ Soon. The danger point has been passed.

♀ An accident will bring you into prominence.

☽ Yes, if you will remember that all things come to him who waits.

♋ Rich in everything excepting money.

♓ Yes, if you can.

♈ Enough to ensure comfort and happiness.

♑ People like yourself always have too many.

♉ He does not understand you at all.

♎ Yes; but give it plenty of consideration.

♂ Quite finish thinking about one thing before you begin to think about another, and all will be well.

♌ Never forget that there is always more room at the top.

♍ Flying.

♐ Just so long as you wish it to be so.

91

The White Magic Book

♃	Across the water, but not far.
♄	For your own sake, do not press for it.
☉	There is something better for you on the same lines.
☿	The one no less than the other.
♀	Do not make any move in the matter, even when opportunity offers.
☽	Not if you take reasonable care of your health in cold weather.
♋	The exact opposite of your own.
♓	Not good-looking but a most attractive personality.
♈	Where he loves, he will trust.
♑	It will be his chief wish.
♉	Yes, if you are careful not to be misunderstood.
♎	A rather unpleasant experience.
♂	You can be, if you wish; but it would be playing with fire.
☊	Petty ones who are everybody's enemies.
♍	Never speculate. In your case it would *eventually* end in disaster.
♐	Country, in the South.

The White Magic Book

♃	There has already been a little.
♄	Yes, but it will lead to much happiness.
☉	You should have done so before.
☿	You will have time to decide what return you will make.
♀	The more delay, the better for everyone concerned.
☽	A few days ago you were together.
♋	You are suspected of knowing too much.
♓	No. It is too late.
♈	That success awaits you very certainly.
♑	Ask. You may safely believe what you will be told.
♉	If you want to, you will. That is your way.
♎	It will be one more experience for you.
♂	Yes, and you will soon have a proof of it.
♌	Is cunning and very quick to grasp an opportunity.
♍	Calmness in the face of misfortune.
♐	Absolutely none.

The White Magic Book

♃	Kindly, on the whole.
♄	You have lost more than you will ever lose in the future.
☉	Yes, very deeply.
☿	You will do well to go no further than the sea-shore.
♀	Yes, you can rely upon that.
☽	You are expected to take the first step toward ending it.
♋	Yes. It will require some effort to keep up with him.
♓	Yes. No one can prevent it.
♈	Good-natured, pretty, and very fond of amusement.
♑	Sooner or later it will come out. Later, if you are careful.
♉	Silence has made you think more than a letter would have done.
♎	Younger than yourself.
♂	Is under the impression that you prefer the society of someone else.
♌	It will be your own until you choose to share it.
♍	Foresight is one of your strong points—make the utmost of it.
♐	The belief that second thoughts are best. You are one who should trust your first impressions.

The White Magic Book

♃   Yes.

♄   Of the last time you were together.

☉   It would be most unwise to do so.

☿   Not unless you define your position clearly and keep to it firmly.

♀   A friend will come to your assistance.

☽   No. You will lose by it and continue to lose.

♋   One, who may cause you trouble.

♓   Always, from first to last.

♈   Good fortune, well deserved.

♑   It is better to bend than to break.

♉   Review your own recent acts and speeches—the explanation is there.

♎   It will be entirely a matter of your choice.

♂   Temporarily, yes.

♌   You will feel that a mansion could not give you truer satisfaction.

♍   The two hundred and seventy-first day of the year.

♐   Not unless you expend much time and trouble over it.

The White Magic Book

♃	Someone has found it.
♄	Not now, but you will live to be envied by many.
☉	No. It would be an unnecessary humiliation.
☿	Yes, and you will regret it for some time to come.
♀	It will come quickly now.
☽	The first emotion cannot last, but there is something far better to come.
♋	Yes, but you will be on the winning side.
♓	You will meet someone who will quite unknowingly be of great use to you.
♈	Be prepared for a great deal of criticism.
♑	Two. Both like yourself.
♉	Neither young nor middle-aged.
♎	Every indication points that way.
♂	It would be a great mistake to try. Wait.
♌	Yes. Steadily and persistently think of what you have to be thankful for.
♍	You will have sufficient means and always be well-liked.
♐	You must reason it out from quite another standpoint.

The White Magic Book

♃	Much more so than it has been so far.
♄	Do not count upon it.
☉	Yes, if you are tired of peace.
☿	That you will be more wise than happy.
♀	That depends upon powers which cannot be influenced.
☽	Yes, as one of a number of associates.
♋	Yes, if you keep calm and refuse to worry.
♓	It is unlikely.
♈	It takes two to make a bargain.
♑	It will be riches to you.
♉	They are prepared for you and you will have to be strong to escape them.
♎	That you think too much about appearances.
♂	You will do so, and it will have far-reaching effects.
♌	Do not try to do more than you have time to do. That is the whole secret.
♍	By never making your grievances a subject of conversation.
♐	It will in some way have to do with machinery.

The White Magic Book

♃	Stay where you are now.
♄	Here.
☉	No. Let sleeping dogs lie.
☿	Yes, but you will have to wait.
♀	The one who is more constantly in your thoughts.
☽	You could if you chose, but it would be better not to do so.
♋	Yes. Be cautious when on stairways.
♓	Brave; and thinks no ill of anyone.
♈	In one whose feelings are very easily hurt.
♑	He could never conceive any reason to be so.
♉	He will do his share. You must do the rest.
♎	Yes, if you are prepared to do all the listening.
♂	Just what generally happens under such circumstances.
♌	Not for some time yet.
♍	Yes, but through no fault of your own.
♐	It makes people strong to fight their own battles sometimes. Leave them to it.

The White Magic Book

♃	If you fear it, you will draw it to you. Cast out fear.
♄	Yes, but few escape that. Ignore it.
☉	There will be more pleasure than sadness for you.
☿	Yes. To know all is to forgive all in this case.
♀	Gifts with a purpose always come too quickly.
☽	It is not a matter of choice, as you know.
♋	You will have to choose between one whom you know and one as yet unknown.
♓	You occupy a position which is desired for someone else.
♈	Do it when you will it will be done too soon.
♑	That you are as good as you are good-looking.
♉	Not now, but may become so.
♎	It bears the impress of truth.
♂	You have trusted others, why not this one?
♌	You would be satisfied if you knew how much.
♍	Has a real gift for talking about nothing.
♐	The lengths to which you will go in the cause of friendship.

The White Magic Book

♃	Your strength of will, which you must not allow to degenerate into obstinacy.
♄	You will have no reason to complain.
☉	Loss of fortune is better than loss of friends, as you will discover later on in life.
☿	Much less so than you think.
♀	Only one, that will cost you a great deal.
☽	That person does not see things in the same way as you do.
♋	Till the end of this moon.
♓	Not the sort of man to be easily deceived.
♈	Yes, if you have sufficient courage and patience.
♑	Naturally very clever, but not highly educated.
♉	It has never really been a secret.
♎	There are more pleasant ways of spending leisure, and some of these have been discovered.
♂	Neither young nor old.
♌	He is more sensitive than you imagine.
♍	You will be the chief influence in it if that is what you mean.
♐	You are very easily swayed by flattery—never trust anyone who offers it to you.